YOU —ON— PURPOSE

YOU ON PURPOSE

ROCKING THIS EARTH-LIFE THING WHILE BECOMING THE PERSON OF YOUR DREAMS

Susie McGann

CFI
An imprint of Cedar Fort, Inc.
Springville, Utah

© 2023 Susie McGann
All rights reserved.

No part of this book may be reproduced in any form whatsoever, whether by graphic, visual, electronic, film, microfilm, tape recording, or any other means, without prior written permission of the publisher, except in the case of brief passages embodied in critical reviews and articles.

This is not an official publication of The Church of Jesus Christ of Latter-day Saints. The opinions and views expressed herein belong solely to the author and do not necessarily represent the opinions or views of Cedar Fort, Inc. Permission for the use of sources, graphics, and photos is also solely the responsibility of the author.

ISBN 13: 978-1-4621-4414-3

Published by CFI, an imprint of Cedar Fort, Inc.
2373 W. 700 S., Suite 100, Springville, UT 84663
Distributed by Cedar Fort, Inc., www.cedarfort.com

Library of Congress Control Number: 2022946435

Cover design by Shawnda T. Craig
Cover design © 2023 Cedar Fort, Inc.

Printed in Colombia

10 9 8 7 6 5 4 3 2 1

Printed on acid-free paper

To the Dormies, for JBs, swinging plungers, Mormonesta Fiestas, random objects, FOP parties, Wally, hats adjourned, marriage lists, bacon nights, and good times past and future.

Contents

Introduction 1

Part 1: Rocking It
The Lame Game 7
Why Not Me? 11
Don't Reach; Increase 17
A Bigger Ball 21
Take the Stairs 27
The Inside Out 33
Shake It Off 37
As You Wish 41
Aspire Higher 45

Part 2: Your Sidekick: Going from Good to Great
The Secret Sauce to an Incredibly Smashing Life 53
Choose Already 59
Attach to God 63
Got SQ? 69
You Are What You Eat 73
The Ram's Way 79
I Choose to Live *Here* 85

Part 3: The Hard Thing about Hard Things
Broken Pieces 97
Miracle Emotions 103

CONTENTS

The Depths of Despair 111
Cut the Shark Music 119
Snip, Snip, Ouch! 125
I Was Born to Do This 131
Be the Good 139

Appendix 143
Bibliography 147
Acknowledgments 161
About the Author 167

Introduction

"We've been stood up." I couldn't believe it. Two impressively hot girls waiting for their promised dates to show up at the door were left with nothing—no notice, no message, just . . . ghosted.

"What punks. Forget them, Kimberly. We are not going to live our lives weeping over the loser choices of others."

And so, we did the only respectable thing any decent young woman could do on a lame, dateless Friday night. We jumped into my neon-green, low-riding 1998 Ford Ranger truck, blasted Kelly Clarkson's "Since U Been Gone," and rode around town with the windows down singing along at full-lung capacity.

Kimberly and I made a pact that day to be Women of Power and Action no matter the lame-os or lame circumstances that came our way.

When you really look at it, our time on this orbiting rock is very short. Most humans have about twenty-eight thousand, four hundred and seventy days to live. If you are female, that amount increases by three percent. If you live in the Bible Belt or grow up in a city, that amount may be smaller.[1] Either way, your days are numbered. Based on Book of Mormon teachings, earth life is a unique time to work, act, and do, but most importantly to change ourselves for the better.[2]

---

1. Leonid A. Gavrilov and Natalia S. Gavrilova, "Predictors of Exceptional Longevity: Effects of Early-Life Childhood Conditions, Midlife Environment and Parental Characteristics," *Living to 100 Monograph* (2014): 1–8. https://www.ncbi.nlm.nih.gov/pmc/articles/PMC4318523/.
2. Alma 42:4: "There was a time granted unto man to repent, yea, a probationary time, a time to repent and serve God."
   Alma 34:32: "This life is the time for men to prepare to meet God; yea, behold the day of this life is the day for men to perform their labors."
   Alma 12:24: "There was a space granted unto man in which he might repent; therefore this life became a probationary state; a time to prepare to meet God."

For a long time, I didn't think much about my power to improve or how to make the most of my time here in Mortalville. All of that changed, however, on Saturday, March 21, 2001, while I was sitting in a non-descript chapel in Woodbridge, Virginia, watching the Young Women general broadcast when President Gordon B. Hinckley gave a talk entitled "How Can I Become the Woman of Whom I Dream?"[3] Among a lot of other blow-your-skirts-off statements, he said, "Limitless is your potential. Magnificent is your future." And then he followed it up with this mic-dropper: "*If* you take control of it."[4]

Although the mic didn't drop, my jaw did. I saw the promise and the risk in that statement. Endless possibilities. Countless opportunities. Immeasurable awesomeness. But it was all up to me. Until that point, I had never considered that so much of my future—even the very person I became—was within my control. I had always figured that I was some fixed quantity and that who I was, was just who I was. President Hinckley opened my eyes to see that so much more lay within my reach.

From that moment on, I became a self-help enthusiast. Over the next years of my life, I frequently found myself standing atop desks or chairs, energetically fist-pumping the air while encouraging my friends and roommates through the ups and downs of our youth-to-adult lives—from getting over those loser boyfriends, to rising above melancholy, to being Women of Power and Action, and to doing The Nephi by Going and Bringing It to Pass. Writing this book has merely been a process of putting on paper the feelings and words that have been exuding out of and stewing within me for many a year now.

The principles I discuss in this book apply to every human—whether you are three or ninety-three. But I wrote this text with beginning-to-be-adult folk in mind, because that's the phase of my life when I saw these principles proven true over and over again. Through

---

3. Gordon B. Hinckley, "How Can I Become the Woman of Whom I Dream?" General Young Women Meeting, April 2001, https://www.churchofjesuschrist.org/study/ensign/2001/05/how-can-i-become-the-woman-of-whom-i-dream?lang=eng.
4. Emphasis added.

INTRODUCTION

the words of prophets, gospel teachings, and lots of seeking, I have learned many strategies to help deal with the hard stuff of life. To come off conqueror. To live deliberately. To grow. I want to share those teachings and my experiences living them with you.

Part 1 of this book is about taking life by the horns and how to let yourself be great unashamedly. This is for those of you who feel that you have more to offer but don't know how to unleash your greatness.

Part 2 reveals how God can multiply your success by infinity. This is for those who feel distanced from God and don't know how to access His life-transforming powers.

Part 3 addresses the challenges that come with trying to do everything discussed in parts 1 and 2. This is for the disillusioned, the heavy hearted, the confused but the seeking.

The last days are here, and the Restoration is unfolding in full force. The need for bold women and men has never been greater. As President Nelson pleaded, we need to speak up and out.[5] In order to do that, our Heavenly Parents need us to know who we are and what we are about. It's not the time to settle for less than what's possible. We each have a birthright, and it is for greatness. Stand up and seize it.

As you make your way through your allocated earth days, the choices that come your way can take you to all-power, all-wisdom, and all-strength, or all-loneliness, all-misery, and all-nothingness. No, you cannot choose much of your circumstances—your skin color, your genes, your parents, your country of origin, how others treat you, who hires you for a job, and so on. But you do choose how you change as you go along. Will you leave better than when you arrived? No one is going to make you improve yourself, least of all your Heavenly Parents. They left any reality of change—the direction and speed—up to you.

---

5. Russell M. Nelson, "A Plea to My Sisters," October 2015 general conference, https://abn.churchofjesuschrist.org/study/general-conference/2015/10/a-plea-to-my-sisters?lang=eng. Russell M. Nelson, "Closing Remarks," April 2019 general conference, https://abn.churchofjesuschrist.org/study/general-conferen ce/2019/04/57nelson?lang=eng.

Part 1
Rocking It

The Lame Game

The day came when the risk to remain tight in a bud was more painful than the risk it took to blossom.[1]

—ELIZABETH APPELL; VOICE OF THUNDER

Keep your head down and don't stand out. That was my mantra for surviving my freshman year of high school. After having spent the previous seven years of my life attending a small, Latter-day Saint private school in central Utah with roughly the same ten kids in my class year after year, my parents moved me across the country the summer before ninth grade and threw me into a large, rowdy *Gentile* public high school.

I was terrified.

My survival technique? Become invisible. Say nothing, do not make eye contact, and hope that no one talks to you. I was very successful at this strategy. No one noticed me. No one ever pointed at me or disagreed with what I said. I was never the laughingstock of the class.

Winning!

NOT.

If you haven't learned this already, the reward for lying low in life is low. I wasn't happy hiding behind a disinterested facade. In fact, I was pretty miserable. I made few friends, opted out of many clubs or

---

1. "Who Wrote 'Risk'? Is the Mystery Solved?" *The Official Anais Nin Blog*, March 5, 2013, http://anaisninblog.skybluepress.com/2013/03/who-wrote-risk-is-the-mystery-solved/.

groups I wanted to be in, and did poorly on several assignments because I was too afraid to raise my hand and ask questions. Every day I went to school I had a choice, and over and over again, I chose to be lame.

Ultimately, the choice to become great, as God intended, or remain lame, as your devil brother wants, is yours. The mandate to "choose ye this day" applies to more than just your religious affiliation.

Do you choose to love yourself or tear yourself to pieces?

Do you choose to live an awesome life or one muddled in mediocrity?

Every moment of growth in your life will be a result of what you have chosen. Even vacillating in indecision is merely the choice to be a passive participant of your circumstance rather than the agent of action God endowed you to be. We think we protect ourselves by playing small, but when we hide our greatness we foolishly trade eventual victory for the enticing ease of surrender.

Like my lame high-school self, Mohandas Gandhi made this same senseless trade over and over again in his early days. Today we know Gandhi as the man who made civil disobedience cool by leading mass peaceful protests against both racism in South Africa and later British rule in India. His courage, wisdom, and can't-stop-this attitude have inspired millions to live their lives deliberately and make big changes with small and simple actions. If you had met Gandhi in his late teens, however, you would never have voted him Most Likely to Succeed. Plagued by self-doubt, anxiety, and social incompetence, he struggled and failed at everything he tried. He barely passed high school and dropped out of college within five months, returning home a hopeless nobody.[2]

In a last-ditch effort to salvage his bleak future, Gandhi's family pulled their meager funds together and paid for him to go to London and study law. He floundered for several months, dealing with the all-too-familiar bouts of fear, social insecurities, and homesickness.[3]

---

2. "Mohandas Karamchand Gandhi," South African History Online, last modified October 9, 2020, https://www.shistory.org.za/people/mohandas-karamchand-gandhi. Eknath Easwaran, *Gandhi the Man: The Story of His Transformation* (California: Nilgiri Press, 1997).
3. Easwaran, *Gandhi the Man*, 16–17.

Yet, slowly, things began to change. During a period of spiritual awakening, Gandhi realized life was passing him by and it was time to take it by the horns. Instead of simply moving along, self-consciously mimicking whatever everyone else was doing, he started making deliberate choices—what to eat, what to wear, how to spend his free time.[4]

When he started his law career in South Africa, he took every case that came to him as an opportunity to grow—no matter how mundane or challenging. As he gained expertise in his work, his self-confidence grew and soon he found himself ready to take on bigger battles that further extended his personal growth. When he was pushed off a South African train for sitting in a white-only section, he decided that instead of returning to India at the end of the year as originally planned, he would stay and fight for the cause of the Indian people, no matter the personal sacrifice that it would entail.[5] His choice to live intentionally and to stand up and stand out again and again not only helped raise himself out of a personal slump of lameness but also empowered others to live boldly and change the world from the inside out.

In this life, God doesn't reward the Play It Safers. He wants men and women of Power and Action who get it done. In the parable of the talents, who is the servant who is rewarded upon the master's return? The man who took a risk and invested the money. In Jesus's ministry, who were the ones who were healed? Those who shouted, pushed through crowds, or broke open rooftops. In the last days, who will be saved? Those who stand boldly by the testimony of Christ.

If you want to make the most of your time here, to become a force to be reckoned with as God intended, you have to be bold. When Paul wanted the Galatians to wake up and drastically change their lives, he reminded them that what they sow, they reap.[6] You won't see big changes in your life if you keep doing the same small-minded things. Staying cloistered in your dorm room yet another Friday night will not lead to you having awesome friendships.

---

4. Easwaran, *Gandhi the Man*, 18–19.
5. South African History Online, "Mohandas Karamchand Gandhi."
6. Galatians 6:7–9.

Opting out of open mic night will not lead to people digging your music. Reciting canned prayers as you drift off to sleep will not lead to powerful spiritual experiences. Quit the lame game. Put your power to choose into action and choose to be awesome. Stand up, stand out, take life by the horns, and go big.

Why Not Me?

*Shoot for the Moon. Even if you miss,
you'll land among the stars.*[1]

—MY FAVORITE QUOTE OF ALL TIME

As you go for bigger and better, you must push yourself to do what you have never done before. In order to do this, you need to have an insane belief in yourself and in your origins and destiny.

David the shepherd boy and his Israelite solider counterparts illustrate the difference that a belief in yourself can make. In that pivotal moment on the battlefield, why did David choose to fight the giant while the others cowered in inaction? Goliath had taunted the Israelite army for forty days. He was rude, and just reading about what he said makes you want to jump in the scriptures and punch him in the face. But not one other solider even attempted a fight. Like David, they assuredly had knowledge of God's power and had been taught of His promise to protect them. Yet, each one underestimated what he was personally capable of and instead focused on irrelevant details: I'm too short. I'm too old. My armor isn't strong enough. I didn't sleep well last night.

What became of these men? What are their names? We don't know. They didn't make it into the Big Book because they let their self-doubt keep them from seizing one of the greatest opportunities of their lives.[2]

---

1. "If I Shoot at the Sun, I May Hit a Star," Quote Investigator, November 20, 2012, https://quoteinvestigator.com/2012/11/20/shoot-at-sun/#note-4805–19.
2. Making it into a history book is not evidence of a life well lived. Millions have come and gone doing wondrous things that were never recorded. But in this case for these men, they had the chance to do something really astounding, and they passed it up because they didn't believe in who they were or what they were capable of.

But David didn't blink an eye at such "facts." He dared to believe he could do the impossible merely because He knew who he was—God's child.[3]

You are not just a human. You are not just a random person who happened to find yourself living on this random planet one day. You are a god in embryo. You existed before coming here. And you will continue to exist after you leave. Although you may not be able to answer *how* you got here, you do know *why* you are here—to become an all-knowing, all-powerful, all-awesomeness being. There are no limits on what is possible because someday, slowly but surely, you are going to be it all, just like Them.

When your Heavenly Mother and Father sent you here, They gave you everything you would need to do and become something great. But at some point along the way, you started believing that what They gave you is not enough.

That you can't.

That you don't have what it takes.

That you aren't cut out for it.

That you'll fail.

These divine-denying lies only grow stronger as you get older. Like the well-worn grooves of habit, the lies increase their hold the more you stay within the bounds they have set persuading you to avoid new or challenging experiences. So you don't go for it. You don't make it happen. You talk yourself out of fighting your giants before you even lift your weapon to try.

Heavenly Mother and Father don't doubt your genes of greatness. Your genes are Their genes. What's more, would They have gone through all the trouble of sending you on this crazy become-gods-like-us

---

3. 1 Samuel 17; 1 Samuel 17:34: "The Lord who rescued me from the paw of the lion and the paw of the bear will rescue me from the hand of this Philistine."
1 Samuel 17:45–46: "You come against me with sword and spear and javelin, but I come against you in the name of the Lord Almighty, the God of the armies of Israel, whom you have defied. This day the Lord will deliver you into my hands."
David was convinced that he didn't need to be stronger or braver or more skilled than Goliath because being God's son, being in His convent, was enough.

journey if They didn't believe you'd come out better on the other end? No way. If They believe in your awesomeness, so can you.

Geneticists and psychologists have tried for years to define human limitations based on genetic makeup, environment, or other definable factors. Yet the only conclusive data they've found is that a person's limits are undefinable. Yes, they can compute a population average. But averages only communicate past data and are poor predictors of future possibilities—especially when it comes to individual achievement.[4] Recent record-breaking physical feats have testified to that fact. The biggest thinkers of the 1800s believed that man as a species could not run faster than a four-minute mile. The human body is not built to exceed that speed, they said. For decades, runners got close to the four-minute mark yet were never able to break through it, further supporting the existence of a biological-derived barrier.[5] That theory was shattered in 1954 by Roger Bannister, who ran it in 3 minutes and 59 seconds.[6] Forty-six days later, another runner ran it in 3 minutes and 58 seconds. The following year, three more runners followed suit, and now hundreds of runners have blazed past the once-thought-impassable-four-minute-mile ceiling.[7]

Much of what holds us back is not our ability but our belief of who we are and what we are capable of.[8] The next time you come up

---

4. David Shenk, *The Genius in All of Us: Why Everything You've Been Told About Genetics, Talent and IQ Is Wrong* (The United States: Double Day, 2010), 65.
5. Neal Bascomb, *The Perfect Mile* (New York: Houghton Mifflin, 2005).
6. Bill Taylor, "What Breaking the 4–Minute Mile Taught Us About the Limits of Conventional Thinking," *Harvard Business Review*, March 9, 2018, https://hbr.org/2018/03/what-breaking-the-4-minute-mile-taught-us-about-the-limits-of-conventional-thinking. Shenk, *The Genius in All of Us*, 31.
7. Even just to qualify for the Olympics in 2020, males need to run the 1500m (.93 miles) in 3 minutes and 35 seconds. Gordon Mack, "2020 Olympic Qualifying Standards Released," *Flotrack*, March 10, 2019, https://www.flotrack.org/articles/6394026-2020-olympic-qualifying-standards-released. A runner's perspective of the mental game required to set a new record: Nathan Brannen, "Only 1,497 Humans Have Ever Broken the 4–minute Mile—and I'm One of Them," *CBC*, June 27, 2018, https://www.cbc.ca/playersvoice/entry/only-1497-humans-have-ever-broken-the-4-minute-mile-and-im-one-of-them.
8. "Science has demonstrated unequivocally that a person's mindset has the power to dramatically affect both short term capabilities and the long-term dynamic of achievement" (Shenk, *The Genius in All of Us*, 89).

with an idea or a goal that intimidates the heck out of you, instead of immediately doubting yourself or letting someone else convince you of all the reasons why you can't do it, think instead, "Why *not* me?" With this one little question, you can blow down walls of limited thinking and open up endless windows of opportunities. By asking, "Why *not* me?" you'll never know how far you will go.

Once you accept the truth that your possibilities are limitless, put all your faith and power into making your *thing* happen. Want to be an Instagram influencer? Go for it. Want to hike the Tokaido Trail? Go for it. Want to audition for the lead role in the community musical? Why not? Your future is as big as your dreams. But no wishful thinking; back those dreams up with work. Energy. Soul power. Let God and everyone else know what your desire is, and show them you mean it by putting in the labor.[9]

I saw the power of this dreaming plus faith action the year I turned nineteen. I had always been mesmerized by foreign travel. The pictures of luscious jungles. The weird and interesting food people ate. The languages they spoke. I loved it all.

But I also believed that foreign travel would never be in the cards for me. That was for rich kids who had resources. I could count the number of times I had been on an airplane with one finger, and I could also count the amount of money I needed to save if I ever wanted to see graduation day at a university. So, when my friends left for study abroad programs and choir tours, I stayed home and went to my minimum-wage job. That is, until one serendipitous afternoon during my Geography 101 class, a guest speaker spoke about a non-profit that sent college kids into developing countries to do humanitarian work.

Like the ocean to Moana, it called me, and I knew I had to go. For the first time I asked myself, "Why *not* me?" Then I got to work. I needed $2,500 plus airfare to get there. I started fundraising. I held yard sales. I washed cars. I hosted dance parties in my dorm room and

---

9. For a deeper dive into the power of dreams, faith, and hard work, pick up a copy of *Think and Grow Rich* by Napoleon Hill. This is an oldie, so some of the language and style is a bit dated. But there's a reason it is still widely read and recommended by some of the most successful people out there.

charged admission. I sent out donor letters to every person I knew asking for money (which was excruciatingly painful, by the way, but I had to show that I wanted it). A month before the trip, I met with the program director to tally up the donations that had come in: $1,956. All my hard work had been for naught—or so I thought. The program director had seen the work I had put in and offered to sponsor the rest of my trip. Three weeks later, I was on a direct flight to San Salvador, a trip that changed the trajectory of my forever.

At the end of your mortal experience, what are you going to regret more? The number of times that you failed to succeed or the number of times that you failed to try? You are an eternal being who will not stop growing until you choose to stop. The only one who sets limits to what you can achieve is you. Your very spiritual makeup was designed with that purpose—to never stop getting better. Even if you fall short of your goal, trying and falling short will always get you farther than not trying at all. As a child of divine beings, you are endowed with the promise of ultimate success. Of greatness. It is your birthright. Stand up, seize it, and get to work.

Don't Reach; Increase

Limitless is your potential.
Magnificent is your future.[1]

—GORDON B. HINCKLEY;
MAN OF GOD, MAN OF WISDOM

As you go about asking the *why not me* question and boldly standing up and out, you can take other actions to more quickly release your powers of awesomeness on your life and the world around you.

How?

Increase your potential: improve yourself, get closer to God, serve others.

How do I know this?

Physics.

I have been fascinated by the idea of potential since I was a Beehive, thanks to the contagious optimism of President Hinckley to "stand a little taller and be a little better."[2] But I have to admit, it's taken me a long time to figure out what potential actually is and how it works.

When we talk about potential, we often use it with the verbs *reach*, *fulfill*, or *realize*. Maybe for this reason, I always imagined that my potential was like a big mason jar that I was trying to fill up. My life substance—or "me," if you will—was the liquid in a half-empty (or is

---

1. Gordon B. Hinckley, "How Can I Become the Woman of Whom I Dream?" General Young Women Meeting, April 2001, https://www.churchofjesuschrist.org/study/ensign/2001/05/how-can-i-become-the-woman-of-whom-i-dream?lang=eng.
2. Gordon B. Hinckley, "Closing Remarks," April 2007 general conference, https://abn.churchofjesuschrist.org/study/general-conference/2007/04/closing-remarks?lang=eng.

it half-full?) mason jar. I imagined it was a sixteen-ounce mason jar, but that my liquidity-substance self only took up about four ounces, leaving twelve empty ounces. The empty space was my "potential." If I worked my hardest and did my bestest, then I could fill the rest of that jar up. Once I got my liquidity-substance self up to the sixteen-ounce line, I would have done it—reached my potential. I also imagined other individuals as liquid substances, floating in jars of all shapes and sizes, some with more or less potential than my twelve ounces of empty space.

Turns out I was wrong. The more I have read about potential energy in the physical realm, coupled with the out-of-this-world promises that God repeatedly bestows upon His children, the more I've realized my mason-jar analogy is lacking. Why? Mason jars are limited—no matter how much I try, how much I learn, or how motivated I am, I will never be able to overflow my mason jar. We know this is not true because God has promised us limitless knowledge, power, and posterity[3]—just like Him. The second fallacy of the mason-jar model is that it's an all-or-nothing game. I've either reached my potential or I haven't. I'm failing until I win.

Potential is not something we reach for but something we increase. Just like physicists describe potential energy in the physical realm, we can increase our personal potential by moving different levers up or down.[4] And if we plan on obtaining godhood someday, increasing our potential is a must.

Potential energy is easy to visualize by imagining a wrecking ball. The larger the wrecking ball, the more potential it has for smashing a building into pieces. The higher up the ball is pulled before it is released, the more potential it has for smashing a building into pieces. Instead of *reaching* your potential, you need to *increase* your potential. You can do this in two ways:

(1) Get a bigger ball. If you want to obliterate an obstacle in your life, instead of repeatedly hitting it with a half-pint wrecking ball, you need to get yourself a bigger ball. You do this by investing in your personal development. At any given time, your potential for impact is

---

3. D&C 132.
4. Specifically gravitational potential energy. Elastic potential energy (for springs or strings) is calculated with a different formula.

equal to "how big of a ball" you are. Your potential for impact grows as you become stronger and more capable. For example, my potential to spread good in the world when I was five was much smaller than it is now. For one, I couldn't read. I didn't know how to use the internet (nor did we have it back then). I only had a close relationship with the seven people in my family and maybe one or two friends from kindergarten. Whether I had wanted to make a positive change in the world around me or not, my potential to do so was pretty small.

Fast forward thirty years and my potential to impact others is much, much greater. For one, I know a lot more. I can read and use the internet. I have met many people and formed personal relationships with them. If I wanted to put a message out to the world, it would reach a thousand or more people through my social media contacts. That's a great deal more than seven.

The self-help world is full of ways to become a bigger ball. Read more. Learn new skills. Meet new people. Exercise. Eat healthy. Whenever you invest in your own capabilities, you increase your potential. The following chapter gives more ideas on how to do this.

(2) Get closer to God. Another way you can increase your potential is to move your position in relation to another object. Keeping with our wrecking-ball metaphor, the higher the crane lifts the wrecking ball up into the sky, the faster and harder it will come flying down toward the doomed building. Likewise, the further we move away from sin and come closer to God, the greater our potential for positive impact. Part 2 of this book goes into more detail on how you can unleash this power in your life.

The more you improve your mind, skills, and talents, and the closer you stick to God, the greater your ability to act and to make a positive difference in the world.

Okay, I'm actually not quite done with my analogy making (isn't science fun?). And this is where the physical world and spiritual world would possibly diverge just a bit. In physics, potential energy is stored—using the energy lowers an object's potential. A read through of the parable of the talents tells us that this is not how it works with people. Saving up your skills, talents, and abilities without putting them to use decreases your potential rather than increases it. In fact, the more you use what you've got, the more you gain. Christ teaches this principle in many places:

- He who makes use of his talents will receive more (see Matthew 25:14–30).
- Unto him that uses his knowledge, God will make wiser (see 2 Nephi 28:30).
- The more you receive and believe, the more you will be given (see Alma 12: 10).
- Speak first, and then the Holy Spirit will guide your words and bear record of what you say (see D&C 100:5–7).

God doesn't bless those who store their potential—so use it!

Understanding our ability to increase our potential in this way should encourage you. We have three avenues of attack to become godly creatures: (1) we can increase our talents and abilities though education, work, and study (improve ourselves); (2) we can grow closer and more committed to God by reading our scriptures, speaking with Him in prayer, and attending His house (strengthen attachment to God); and (3) we can put our hearts and minds to work by using our gifts and talents for good (serve others). Doing just one of these strategies will increase our potential. Doing all three will elicit a personal typhoon of greatness.

We are not just creatures of growth; we are creatures of transformation. Even evolution testifies to that fact. It may still be up for debate whether or not man once came from apes. However, what's more incredible—that an ape can become a man, or a man can become a god? What you are capable of today does not reflect what you will be capable of tomorrow. Christ's arms are outstretched still,[5] inviting you to believe in the power of change and to allow Him to transform you into a new creature.[6]

---

5. 2 Nephi 19:21.
6. Mosiah 27:25–26.

A Bigger Ball

Those who accomplish the most in this world
are those with a vision for their lives.[1]

—M. RUSSELL BALLARD; A MAN BUILT UPON A ROCK

Increasing your potential will take time, and the only way you will find the time to do it is to make time. How? Get picky about your priorities and ruthless about your early mornings. Yes, M-O-R-N-I-N-G-S, that time of the day that you usually sleep through. Wake up early in the morning and set it apart for one thing—to become better.

During the day, we have so much to get done that we have little to no spare time to consciously spend on becoming stronger, smarter, better. Daytime is go time. But the early morning can become your Improve You Time. You are only capable of so much now. But as you work on *you*, you become capable of so much more. If mornings just don't work for you, find time every day to set apart for personal improvement.

Whenever you decide to hold daily Improve You Time, divide your time block into two parts: visualize and execute.

Visualize. Imagine it to life.

If you want to create something, you need to spend time imagining what it is going to look like and how you are going to achieve it. Everything that you see around you came to exist in the tangible

---

1. M. Russell Ballard, "Return and Receive," April 2017 general conference, https://www.churchofjesuschrist.org/study/general-conference/2017/04/return-and-receive?lang=eng.

world after it was first created in the mental world. This is the same pattern God used to create the earth as described in Genesis and the Pearl of Great Price. He imagined every detail—how water would change form and progress through the various elements of earth and sky, how the wings of the insects would buzz as they moved, how the digestive systems of animals would sustain certain food sources.

The evidence that a spiritual creation precedes a physical one abounds. Athletes in particular have perfected this science. Before every meet, Michael Phelps, twenty-three-time gold medalist (the most gold medals ever won by a single person), closes his eyes and imagines himself walking to the pool, lining up at the start, leaping into the water in a perfect dive, and taking stroke after stroke in perfect form. It is only after he has visualized a perfect execution that he is able to execute perfectly.[2]

If you do not have a vision for your life or even your day, chances are you are realizing the vision of someone else.[3] Habitually flipping to Hulu as soon as you get home from work plays right into the vision Hulu's marketing team spent millions of dollars refining. Filling your Amazon cart chock-full of things you don't need nor really even want carries out the meticulously crafted vision of Amazon's product managers. Scrolling through your social media feed for unknown amounts of time while in the bathroom fulfills the detailed vision of Twitter's UI designers. Even listening to those less-than-godly urges to mock people under your breath when you feel offended satisfies the vision your dark side relations stay up at night gleefully imagining. While you mindlessly drift from this to that, high-fives are being passed around elsewhere because someone just got you to do exactly what they planned, visualized, and hoped for.

---

2. *The Washington Post,* "Olympics 2012: Michael Phelps Has Mastered the Psychology of Speed," YouTube video, 3:22, June 15, 2012, https://www.youtube.com/watch?v=Htw780vHH0o. Olivier Poirier-Leroy, "How Michael Phelps Used Visualization to Stay Calm Under Pressure," YourSwimBook, accessed February, 17, 2021, https://www.yourswimlog.com/michael-phelps-visualization/.

3. Stephen R. Covey, *The Seven Habits of Highly Effective People: Powerful Lessons in Personal Change* (New York: Fireside, 1989), 81–94.

Don't realize someone else's dream. Create your own vision for your life, get specific about it, and spend time each day perfecting and imagining it.

Suggestions to help you craft your vision:

- Start with crafting a long-term, broad vision and then work backwards, visualizing more specific, short-term events. Make sure your broad vision includes a holistic look at your life. Include physical, spiritual, mental, and social aspects of the future you.
- Reflect on how things are going and what things you want to change.
- Meditate and explore possibilities. (Don't limit yourself; ask the *why not me* question.)
- Pray and ask for your Heavenly Parents to help you craft a vision of yourself. Study your patriarchal blessing—it's a gold mine for inspiration.
- When you decide on a goal you want to go for, explore every angle about that idea. Ask, *how*, *where*, and *when*, and then find the answers. Research will help your vision become more realistic, detailed, and thus, doable.

You won't be able to visualize some things because you don't know the details yet. It's less important that your vision include the weight, height, and hair color of your future spouse and more important that it include you in a loving, secure, committed relationship.

Once you've honed the *what* of your vision, write it down or make a vision board, and put it where you can see it regularly. Spend time every morning closing your eyes and going over your vision. Make your mental images as vivid as possible. Internalize it. Breathe it. Become it.

I can't stress enough how much imagining your future reality works. When I was finishing graduate school, I had a strong desire to speak at graduation. I wasn't an exceptional student nor a particularly interesting person, but why not me? Public speaking was a skill I wanted to get better at, and my vision of my future self included speaking to large crowds of people. Not only that, but the idea scared the pants off me. I had to do it. To make my desire known, I told God and sent an email to an advisor in my college, telling him I was interested in speaking and asking how the selection process worked. I never heard back from the advisor (it turned out he didn't work at the university anymore), but a few months later I received an email saying I had been nominated by my department to participate in graduation. If I wanted to be the student speaker, I needed to fill out an application and write a three-hundred-word blurb of what I would speak to my fellow graduates about. I spent the next few weeks using whatever spare moment I had to visualize what I would say. When I had a vision I was happy with, I wrote it down and submitted it. A few weeks later, I received word that I had been selected as the student speaker. But my vision work was far from over.

During the weeks leading up to convocation, I imagined and re-imagined the big day, from what shoes I would wear to where I would sit on the stage. I envisioned where in the speech I would turn my head to the left or right, where I would pause for effect, or when I would take a breath. Two days before, I visited the Marriott Center and practiced what I had envisioned on the empty stage. I practiced sitting down, standing up, walking to the pulpit, and giving my speech—over and over again. The janitors on shift probably thought I was crazy. I didn't care. This was my time to act, and I knew that the more detailed my vision was, the better I could realize it.

When the day of convocation arrived, it was like running a script. I hardly had to think about what I was doing. I felt comfortable and prepared. Every minute detail I had envisioned came true.

This. Stuff. Works.

Execute. Get up and bring it to pass.

After you've invested some of your Improve You Time into creating a vision, leave time for the doing. If your vision involves you hitting a new PR on the treadmill, spend time at the gym. If your vision includes you swooning the girl next door, plan your next move. If your vision includes a secure relationship with God, pick up those scriptures. Since your vision should be a holistic view of your future self, make deposits in every aspect of your life. Your Improve You

Time should leave you a little stronger physically, socially, spiritually, and mentally. Some ideas include:

- **Exercise.** Your body is your vehicle. Don't wait until the oil light is blinking before you give it some TLC. You don't need to win any medals; just take care of yourself.
- **Meditate.** David O. McKay called mediation the language of the soul[4] long before it was cool. Check in with your mind. Find a quiet spot and just sit with yourself for a moment of gratitude and acceptance.
- **Read.** It doesn't matter what it is just as long as it is quality. What's quality? It's uplifting and teaches you something. When was the last time you read something that wasn't required or the result of click bait? The number of must-read books are endless. Biographies and Harvard classics are good places to start. Or, for other recommendations, browse the footnotes of general conference talks. Our leading brothers and sisters are well read.[5] Reading expands your mind like nothing else. Do it every day.
- **Write.** This could be your thoughts, goals, or what you did yesterday. Writing is practice getting out of you what is within you. It clarifies thinking, expands reasoning powers, soothes the soul, and ingrains ideas into long-term memory.[6] Don't get too hung up on what to write. Start with a brain dump where you merely scribble down whatever comes into your mind. Your thoughts will slowly gravitate to a particular point or topic that your subconscious needs to bring to the surface.
- **God time.** You can accelerate your personal growth by coming closer to God. Spend time with Him every day.

---

4. The Church of Jesus Christ of Latter-day Saints, *Teachings of the Presidents of the Church: David O. McKay* (Salt Lake City: The Church of Jesus Christ of Latter-day Saints, 2011), 31–32, https://abn.churchofjesuschrist.org/study/manual/teachings-david-o-mckay/chapter-4?lang=eng.
5. Visit susiemcgann.com for some of my recommended reads.
6. Extra benefit if you write by hand with a pencil and a paper. Sounds crazy, but for reals. Mix up your life and write it on paper. Take the time to form your letters neatly. Learn (or relearn) cursive. You'll fall in love with it.

You won't be able to spend considerable time on improving yourself every morning, but do something every day, even if it's just five minutes.[7] If you don't have as much time one morning, still do something, even if it's just one minute per item. This will help you stay in the habit of self-improvement.

As you make time to improve yourself on a consistent basis, you will exponentially increase your ability to rock it.[8] In 2019 I started tracking my Improve You Time to up my accountability and make sure I was doing something every day to improve myself. My potential to go and do skyrocketed. I wrote for fifteen minutes every day and completed and published an article in a peer-reviewed journal. I posted on social media three to five times a week and slowly grew a following from nonexistent to not-too-shabby. I exercised four days a week and completed two five-minute plank challenges. I prayed and studied my scriptures daily and improved my relationship with my Heavenly Parents. I reflected on the positive characteristics of my One and Only, and my love for him grew.

Your limits are endless, *if* you take control of it. Give yourself time every day to become more.

---

7. James Clear, the author of *Atomic Habits,* suggests that doing a small action consistently pays bigger dividends than doing an action hardcore every once in a while. James Clear, *Atomic Habits: An Easy & Proven Way to Build Good Habits & Break Bad Ones* (New York: Avery, 2018).
8. Want to really rock your Improve You Time? Hal Elrod walks you through the steps on how to set up a morning routine that will transform you, one break-of-dawn at a time. Hal Elrod, *The Miracle Morning: The Not-So-Obvious Secret Guaranteed to Transform Your Life (Before 8AM)* (Hal Elrod International, Inc., 2019).

Take the Stairs

*I am not afraid of storms,
for I am learning how to sail my ship.*[1]

—LOUISA MAY ALCOTT;
AUTHOR, CHAMPION OF WOMEN, GOD-FEARER

After my best friend, Becky, and I were cut from our high school musical tryouts (no vocal talent, apparently), we decided to join the cross country team. We both played lacrosse in the spring, so we thought prepping our legs in the fall would give us a leg up. And how bad could it be; it was just running, right?

Little did I know that cross country means to run and keep running after any sane person would have stopped. And unlike in lacrosse or other sane-people sports, you don't run to catch something, like a ball or a person with a ball. You just run to run. As if blessed by the gods, my normally weekend-only job occasionally scheduled me to work during the week, which kept me from going to practices now and then. I welcomed the alibi. When my team went to run hills or train on the off-road course, I was more than pleased to ride off to work and sit in my comfy chair stuffing little kids' next best friends at Build-A-Bear Workshop®. I missed three practices a month and quickly became the slowest person on the team. The gap between my strength and that of my teammates became embarrassingly apparent at Districts where Becky, who had matched me stride for stride in September, zoomed past me with ease. When I rolled my ankle halfway through the third

---

1. Louisa May Alcott, *Little Women*, (Project Gutenberg, 1996, Last updated April 3, 2020), https://www.gutenberg.org/cache/epub/514/pg514–images.html.

mile, "Thank you, God" were the first words out of my mouth. I now had an excuse to sit out for the rest of the season.

During that miserable cross country season, I learned about the relationship between growth and struggle. I skipped out on the struggle and in turn lost out on the growth. This principle doesn't just govern athletes training for a race but all of God's creations. Physics expresses this truth as "an object in motion will stay in motion unless acted upon by an outside force." And we see the long-term consequences of struggle and growth play out in biology through natural selection and evolution. Regardless of nature's canny ability to help organisms become super adept at surviving, she can only release this perfecting power when significant opposition exists (an outside force), whether that be extreme environments or aggressive predators. If that weren't so, we would see a lot more invincible species walking around. Consider the honeybee, for example. That little stinger of his is pretty darn powerful. But in terms of its value to the survival of the species, it comes with an obvious limitation: to sting is to die. Why hasn't natural selection helped the honeybee develop a stinger that it can use to protect itself *and* live to tell the tale? This puzzled Darwin, too. Then he realized, "Natural selection tends only to make each organic being as perfect as, or slightly more perfect than the other inhabitants of the same country with which it comes into competition."[2] Translation: Once the struggle to survive ceases, so does the growth.

God uses external forces to propel us toward perfection as well. When He was helping the Jaredites get to the promised land, He didn't put them on a cloud and coast them gently over like a modern-day Carnival cruise ship. Instead, He "caused that there should be a furious wind blow upon the face of the waters." This wind was so fierce and powerful that it caused "mountain waves" and "great and

---

2. Charles Darwin, *On the Origin of Species* (London: John Murray, 1872; Project Gutenberg, 1999), chapter 6. https://www.gutenberg.org/files/2009/2009-h/2009-h.htm. Although Darwin discusses the honeybee example in his work, I first read about it and Darwin's explanation in Givens and Givens, *The God Who Weeps*, 61–62.

terrible tempests" to break upon them so that they were "tossed upon the waves of the sea."[3]

Seems kinda extreme. But here's the key part: all of this storm and fury were consistent in one thing—direction. "And it came to pass that the wind did never cease to blow towards the promised land."[4] He used the winds (force, pressure, and opposition) to get the people closer to their end goal—a better place.

No need to wait for the Man Upstairs to send growth-propelling forces your way or for some tragic disaster to hit. You can quicken personal growth by intentionally making your life harder. I know it sounds crazy, but in today's world, the easiest option is often the default option. We spend most of our lives in climate-controlled buildings and vehicles. We explore new places without ever getting lost, thanks to GPS. We eat a variety of foods we don't have to make or even leave our house to get. If we don't deliberately add some challenge to the mix, we are in serious risk of ending up like the fictional human population depicted in the Pixar movie *WALL-E*—fat, babied, and atrophied.

To keep yourself in growth mode, aim to spend as much time as possible in the *i*+1 zone; *i* being your current level of ability and +1 being slightly beyond what you are capable of. For example, if you want to learn a new language, you need to listen to or read texts that are one step above your current ability. Texts that are two or more above your *i* will be frustrating and discouraging, but texts at or below your *i* will be boring and, in terms of growth, useless.[5]

You don't need to do anything extreme. Just look for little ways to add that +1 to your life. Mix up your routine and drive without air conditioning. Sleep on the floor. Seek out uncomfortable social situations. Volunteer to do something that terrifies you. Stoics of the ancient world believed that deliberately making your life uncomfortable now and then would not only make you stronger but

---

3. Ether 6:5–6.
4. Ether 6:5, 8.
5. Steven Brown and Jenifer Larson-Hall, *Second Language Acquisition Myths: Applying Second Language Research to Classroom Teaching* (Michigan: University of Michigan, 2012), 60–61.

also prepare you to better handle life's unexpected challenges.[6] Seneca purportedly wore ridiculous clothes in public so that he could practice feeling shame and ridicule.[7] Others chose to go shoeless around town or wear light clothing on a cold night to practice being physically uncomfortable. Pleasure haters? No. Self punishers? No. They merely saw the strengthening power in adversity and wanted to expedite the fruits as much as possible.

In addition to increasing the reading on your I-can-do-this barometer, adding difficulty to your life can enhance your sense of meaning. Wasn't this the desire that lured Adam and Eve into kicking off this mortal experience for us all? Think about it: Adam and Eve lived in paradise. They didn't need to do any type of work. They could sleep in late, idle around, eat all they wanted, and never had to worry about where to be or what to wear. Could it have been that, along with Eve's quick calculations of how to comply with commandment number two, they were just bored? Or, more eloquently stated, unfulfilled?[8]

Yet again, I learned this the hard way in high school, this time when picking my school schedule. I had taken AP classes since freshman year and was very comfortable with the pace and expectations of those courses. But AP English Literature was a different story; all of the seniors said so anyway. For one, it was taught by Ms. Scharl. She meant business and didn't forgive late work. Students had to read fifteen novels throughout the year, which averaged to about one thousand pages a week. There was no way I could keep up with that!

---

6. William B. Irvine, *A Guide to the Good Life: The Ancient Art of Stoic Joy* (New York: Oxford University, 2008), chapter 7, Kindle. As Seneca said, "If you would not have a man flinch when the crisis comes, train him before it comes." Lucius Annaeus Seneca, *Letters from a Stoic: All Three Volumes,* trans. Richard Mott Gummere (Enhanced Media, 2015), 41, ebook.
7. Irvine, *A Guide to the Good Life*, chapter 7.
8. Erling Kagge introduced me to this perspective of the Adam and Eve story. In this podcast interview he talks about other benefits of struggle and seeking out regular challenges (see Erling Kagge, "Podcast #560: The Magic of Walking," interview with Brett McKay, *The Art of Manliness*, podcast audio, November 13, 2019, https://www.artofmanliness.com/articles/benefits-of-walking/).

So I skipped it. I didn't sign up. And all year I sat reading watered-down easy readers in a class where it didn't matter if I had a pulse. As I strained to keep my eyelids open and refrain from bashing my head against the wall in pursuit of some kind of mental stimulation, my friends spent the semester reading the great classics of the ages, discussing ideas, formulating thoughts, polishing essays (and, yes, reading Spark Notes), but all in all they were having a much more meaningful experience than I was.

Balance applies here just like in any life approach. Not everyone needs to take the same classes or follow the same fitness schedule to feel challenged and fulfilled. As King Benjamin reminds us, don't run faster than you have strength.[9] But are you avoiding challenges out of self-awareness, or out of fear? Reconfiguring your association of "hard = bad" and "easy = good" will allow you to explore new opportunities that you may have run away from before. This is the big point that the one-third who left God's presence so early in the game missed. They wanted the easier path without realizing that they were really choosing the impossible path. Without struggle, there is no growth.

---

9. Mosiah 4:2.

The Inside Out

*Whatever you become,
you become in your head first.*[1]

—ORACENE PRICE; MOTHER EXTRAORDINAIRE TO
TENNIS SUPERSTARS VENUS AND SERENA WILLIAMS

The summer I flew back from my humanitarian trip in El Salvador, I got a job selling pest control door to door. I was stoked about the pay but not so stoked about the idea of being an annoying, pesky solicitor. Would people yell at me? Slam the door in my face? Hide behind their curtains when they saw me coming? Worried that the inevitable onslaught of negativity would slacken my resolve and make me quit my golden-egg job prematurely, I made a plan. I would zap others' negative thoughts with positive thoughts of my own. I covered my bedroom walls with notes shouting positive affirmations such as, "You can do this!" "Don't give up!" "Solicitors are people too!"

Instead of tracking how many doors I knocked, I kept a running list of interesting people I met or highlights of my day. Crazily enough, my plan worked. Instead of hating my job, I loved it! Instead of sucking at door-to-door sales, I rocked! I made friends in whatever neighborhood I worked, and although I wasn't the highest earning rep in the office, I was the only one who worked the whole summer without one single bagel (rep lingo for a no-sales day).

It was from this experience and others like it that I learned how our thoughts influence our achievements and progress. If you want to get to the point where you can bravely ask the *why not me* question,

---

1. Karlin Gray, *Serena: The Littlest Sister* (Massachusetts: Page Street Kids, 2019), 10.

seek out growth-hacking situations, and increase your potential, you need to start taking control of what happens between your two ears. Mind-blowing, divine origins aside, if you tell yourself you are lousy, you will do lousy things and feel lousy. If you tell yourself you are not worth loving, you will be hard pressed to find a thing you love about yourself. On the other hand, if you tell yourself you are awesome and are capable of doing a million wonderful things, your chances of making them come to pass just quadrupled by a million.

Even just changing the verbs you use can make a big difference in your day-to-day success. Dr. Susan Jeffers found that certain words create feelings of power and others of helplessness.[2] For example, feel the difference between saying *I can't* and *I won't* when telling your friends about your behavior choices: I *can't* go out tonight because I work in the morning, versus, I *won't* go out tonight because I work in the morning.[3] Do you feel it? One answer cedes to an external force acting upon you and controlling your behavior, while the other places you in full control of your decision.

If you want to dictate the direction of your life, start using words that mirror a powerful mindset.

Other I'm-a-victim-of-my-life-and-I-can't-do-anything-about-it phrases that you can replace with Words of Power include:

- I should vs. I could
- It's not my fault vs. I'm totally responsible
- It's a problem vs. It's an opportunity
- Nothing makes me happy vs. I find joy where I look for it

---

2. Susan Jeffers, *Feel the Fear . . . and Do It Anyway* (New York: Ballantine Books, 1987), 31. The list of power terms and their counterparts also comes from her book, although I have modified some of them.
3. Real-life example: In an auditorium of 400 young men, a presenter asked how many had pornography on their devices. All of the boys raised their hands except three. When asked why they didn't look at pornography, two of the boys said, "We're Mormons. We're not allowed to have porn." The last boy responded, "I'm evangelical Christian. I believe Jesus Christ is my Lord and Savior, and I don't think He'd want me to mess with porn." Which boy do you think is going to live his life on purpose, and which do you think are going to end up feeling victimized and powerless? (See Leonard Sax, *Boys Adrift: The Five Factors Driving the Growing Epidemic of Unmotivated Boys and Underachieving Young Men* [New York: Basic Books, 2016], 172–173).

- Life's a struggle vs. Life's an adventure
- I hope vs. I know
- If only vs. Next time
- What will I do? vs. I can handle this
- It's terrible vs. It's a learning experience

Use your words to keep yourself in the driver seat of your life. When you use words of helplessness, you turn off your ability to utilize the go-and-do power God has given you. Remember, you were made to act, not to be acted upon.[4]

The words we think do more than change the vibes in our mind space; they also change the physical structure of our brains. You heard that right. The words you think change the shape and form of your brain. Meditation, for example, triggers many tangible, observable changes in the brain. One study on Rajyoga meditation found that participants who spent time focusing thoughts on positive attributes or themes such as peace, love, or joy grew a surprising amount of brownish-gray tissue in their brain compared to those who did not meditate.[5] Despite how it sounds, this gray matter is a good thing. The more gray matter you have, the better your brain functions, makes decisions, handles stress, learns new skills, and regulates emotions. When Mosiah told us to "watch your thoughts and your words,"[6] he was teaching us the secret to change from the inside out.

Mastering control over your thoughts can also help you see ways to improve your life that you never recognized before. True, you will never be able to change some things in your life, but by focusing on that stuff, you'll never see the opportunities to do the things you can control. Stephen R. Covey excelled at teaching people this concept in his book *The Seven Habits of Highly Effective People*. (Thirty years later,

---

4. 2 Nephi 2:14, 16: "For there is a God, and he hath created all things, both the heavens and the earth, and all things that in them are, both things to act and things to be acted upon.... Wherefore, the Lord God gave unto man that he should act for himself."
5. Ramesh Babu MG, Rajagopal Kadavigere, Prakashini Koteshwara, Brijesh Sathian, and Kiranmai S. Rai, "Rajyoga Meditation Experience Induces Enhanced Positive Thoughts and Alters Gray Matter Volume of Brain Regions: A Cross-sectional Study" *Mindfulness* 12 (2021): 1659–1671, https://doi.org/10.1007/s12671-021-01630-8.
6. Mosiah 4:30.

it is still in the Top Twenty Most Popular Books sold in bookstores.)[7] In his book, Covey teaches you to imagine two circles: one circle drawn around all the stuff that is within your control to change, and the other drawn around all the stuff that you can't control. Which circle is bigger?

Unless you are God, the latter circle will be tremendously bigger. But here's the surprising thing—the more you focus on the circle containing the stuff that you can control, the larger that circle grows. This phenomenon is similar to how your eyes bring objects into focus. When your eyes focus on an object, whether the object is close or far away, your eyes blur everything else out in order to more clearly define what you are looking at. Although the focused object doesn't change physical size, it captures more of your mental awareness than if it were blurred or in the background, and as a result, you are able to see details of line and shadow that you weren't able to see before. The same effect happens when you focus your mental energy on certain thoughts or ideas. Focusing on things within your control amplifies them and allows you to see possibilities you would never have recognized before, while at the same time, blurring out the depressing deluge of distractions that you really can't do anything about anyway.

It was this thought-focusing power that the Prophet Joseph Smith urged the Saints to use in the midst of their darkest hour of persecution. Persecution so horrific and vile that Joseph claimed it made "hell itself shudder . . . and the hands of the very devil to tremble and palsy."[8] Talk about rights to a pity party. Yet, the Prophet would not let the Saints wallow in the outer circle of helplessness. He encouraged them to stay focused on what they could do while not fretting about the rest: "Therefore, dearly beloved brethren, let us cheerfully do all things that lie in our power; and then may we stand still, with the utmost assurance, to see the salvation of God, and for his arm to be revealed."[9]

---

7. Covey, *The Seven Habits of Highly Effective People*, 81–94.
8. D&C 123:10.
9. D&C 123:15. Affirmations are an excellent way to initiate change from the inside out. A book I highly recommend to get you into the habit of reciting affirmations on a daily basis is *The Greatest Salesman in the World* by Og Mandino. I use some of the affirmations provided in his book word for word, and other times I use them as guidelines to make my own. The inner story of the book reminds us that the greater reason we strive for excellence in all we do is to glorify and honor Him.

Shake It Off

Don't let the Muggles get you down.[1]
—RON WEASLEY; FRIEND, FIGHTER, CONQUEROR

As you're out there doing your rock-this-life thing, you are going to run into haters—people who want to tear down or slow down your man-to-god process. Ignore them. Their hate has nothing to do with you.

I learned this truth unintentionally my freshman year of college when I ran into a hater. I was studying in my dorm room when I decided to take a break and get some fresh air. I walked out to the second story veranda, took a deep breath of the cool autumn air, and enjoyed the feeling of the breeze blow through my I-need-a-haircut-but-can't-afford-it-cuz-I'm-a-starving-student long hair. As I was standing on the balcony, a girl sitting with a group of people from my ward made the mocking remark, "Rapunzel, Rapunzel, let down your hair." I suppose I did look a little ridiculous leaning into the wind and taking in air like a prisoner locked in a tower. But I was surprised and embarrassed to be the target of someone else's joke. Somehow, I played it off like I didn't hear, soaked in one last breath, and then, with all my princess airs, walked off the balcony and went back inside. Despite my insecurities, I shrugged off the remark as an expression of jealousy for my gorgeous locks and didn't think much of it again.

A few months later, when everyone in the dorms was moving out for the summer, the girl who had made the remark showed up at my door and apologized for being mean to me that semester. Apparently,

---

1. J.K. Rowling, *Harry Potter and the Prisoner of Azkaban* (New York: Scholastic Inc., 1999), 10.

she had said a fair number of negative comments about me behind my back. I'd had no idea. Besides the Rapunzel remark, I wasn't even aware that she knew who I was. When she asked for forgiveness, I realized that while I had been doing my thing and enjoying it, she had spent the same time weighed down with the mental and emotional baggage that comes from dwelling on other people's lives. If I had known the extent of the gossip, it would have been hard to ignore and maybe even to forgive. But it was empowering to realize that people's hate only has power over me if I give it to them. Otherwise, it's their problem, not mine.

People who stand up and live bold will receive hate, criticism, or disapproval of some kind at some point. It's inevitable. Take Abraham Lincoln, for example. Today, we think he's the hottest thing since democracy. He's been voted the most popular US president for decades, outranking FDR, Jefferson, even Washington.[2] But, sheesh, did he have a lot of haters in his day.

"Idiot."

"The original gorilla."

"Weak as water."

"Timid, vacillating, and inefficient."[3]

That's a sampling of the acidic wordage he was bombarded with on a daily basis. And that's just from the Republicans! I won't repeat what the Southerners called him. One of his closest advisors said he "lacks practical talent for his important place" and did not nominate him for reelection. Ouch. The pressure to give up, throw in the towel, curl up into a ball, and cry was strong, and he definitely wasn't immune to it. After reading an especially cutting critique in the paper, he allegedly cried out, "I would rather be dead than, as president, thus abused in the house of my friends."

---

2. "Presidential Historians Survey 2021," C-SPAN, accessed October 2021, https://www.c-span.org/presidentsurvey2021/?page=overall.
3. Mark Bowden, "'Idiot,' 'Yahoo,' 'Original Gorilla': How Lincoln Was Dissed in His Day: The difficulty of recognizing excellence in its own time," *The Atlantic*, June 2013, https://www.theatlantic.com/magazine/archive/2013/06/abraham-lincoln-is-an-idiot/309304/.

The hate and put-downs and mockery are, unfortunately, a built-in feature of this mortal life. Like the big and spacious building in Lehi's dream, people's verbal attacks are often Big Bad Bro's most powerful tool in diverting us from getting through this life bigger and better and closer to our Heavenly Parents than before.

More devastating than making you a target of others' ridicule, however, is persuading you to join the haters in the taunting brawl. Leading a life of negativity leads nowhere. Think about it—what are the mocking people in the large and extensive edifice doing? Mocking! They are not walking or building or growing or doing anything even bucket-list worthy. Rather, they are choosing to spend precious hours of their lives obsessing over and complaining about someone else's.

An Indian fable illustrates the self-destructive nature of retaliating to haters while on your life journey. In the story, a tortoise overhears two geese talking about their luscious homeland in the Himalayas, and he begs them to take him along.

"Sure, we'll take you!" they say. "Grab onto the end of this stick with your mouth and we'll each take a side with our big talon feet."

The animals got situated and then took off. And oh, what a beautiful ride. Who knew the earth looked so green and peaceful from the air?

"I'm so lucky," the contented turtle thought.

As the trio flew over a village, a group of kids saw them and started pointing and laughing at the unusual sight.

"How ridiculous! A flying turtle! Kinda bald for a bird aren't you, Tortoise?!"

Well, Mr. Tortoise was not going to have any of that. He opened his mouth to give those pestering twerps a piece of his mind. But of course, when he started to speak, he lost hold of the stick and plummeted down, down, down to the ground, gratifying his tormentors with the world's first turtle soup.[4]

When we receive hate from the critics in our lives, remembering whose opinion matters and whose doesn't is the best way to ignore

---

4. A good scripture that drives the point home is 1 Peter 3:7: "For it be better if the will of God be so that ye suffer for well doing, than for evil doing."

the cacophony of dissenters and tune in to the one voice that actually counts—God's.

Why is God's voice the most important? Because what He thinks is always true. What other people think may or may not be. Taking suggestions from people who give you wrong directions will not help you progress on your journey of greatness. Not that other people can't give us needed feedback sometimes. Maybe Lincoln was a little on the timid side. But not to the point that he needed to step down from his presidency. If you allow God's voice to be loudest in your life, you will never run the risk of letting false ideas dictate your rumbo and as a result miss out on the greatest victories of your existence. It was Lincoln's relentless pursuit of God's will versus popularity that helped him lead our quarreling nation unapologetically forward instead of caving into the cries to quit from the convinced, yet misguided, peanut gallery.[5, 6]

Don't waste your time with the gossipers, haters, or cynics out there. Their negativity is their own punishment. Don't let it spread to you. You'll never be able to soar by judging other people. You only get one chance at this earth-life thing. Just do you.

---

5. The Abraham Lincoln Association, ed., *Collected Works of Abraham Lincoln. Volume 5* (Ann Arbor, Michigan: University of Michigan Digital Library Production Services, 2001), 419–420, accessed April 26, 2022, https://quod.lib.umich.edu/cgi/t/text/text-idx?c=lincoln;cc=lincoln;type=simple;rgn=div1;q1=September%2013,%201862;view=text;subview=detail;sort=occur;idno=lincoln5;node=lincoln5:933. An example of Lincoln's internal dialogue when presented with differing opinions and how he ultimately tried to find God's will, or ultimate truth, upon which to base his decisions: pages 419–420: "I am approached with the most opposite opinions and advice, and that by religious men, who are equally certain that they represent the Divine will. I hope it will not be irreverent for me to say that if it is probable that God would reveal his will to others, on a point so connected with my duty, it might be supposed he would reveal it directly to me; for, unless I am more deceived in myself than I often am, it is my earnest desire to know the will of Providence in this matter. *And if I can learn what it is I will do it!* These are not, however, the days of miracles, and I suppose it will be granted that I am not to expect a direct revelation. I must study the plain physical facts of the case, ascertain what is possible and learn what appears to be wise and right."

6. A scriptural example of tuning into God's voice over your critics is Nephi the First. Can you imagine if he hadn't stepped up his game and gotten the plates, crafted the bow, built the boat, or made flipping Nephite history because he let his brothers' naysaying matter more to him than what God told him was possible?

As You Wish

Our desires . . . lie at the core of our very souls.[1]
—NEAL A. MAXWELL; SPIRITUAL DYNAMITE INCARNATE

I don't say this to brag, but in my early twenties, I was pretty cute. I had style. And it was a unique, this-is-me style. I had mastered the art of throwing together avant garde outfits out of stellar clearance finds and my sisters' hand-me-downs. I had painstakingly crafted every word of my Facebook bio and hand coded my Myspace page to auto play my favorite song all while showcasing my favorite photos of my cute self doing fun things with my friends. I knew exactly who I was, and I had a whole slew of online content to prove it.

Fast forward two years to me slogging through the muddy streets of Uruguay as a newly christened missionary with runny nylons, frumpy skirts, and embarrassingly hairy legs to boot. I felt that my "identity" had been obliterated by a professional-grade bulldozer. My shoes, clothes, music, friends, and this-is-me stuff were suddenly stripped away, and I was left with nothing tangible to point to that defined who I was. This sudden I-am-living-a-different-life experience taught me a pretty significant lesson: I am not my clothes. In fact, I wasn't who I thought I was at all. When I peeled back the layers of what I had assumed represented my identity, I found that under it all lay one thing—my desires.

Our desires are like the gusts of wind in the sails that guide our lives to a destination. Our desires determine what clothes we put on

---

1. Neal A. Maxwell, "Swallowed Up in the Will of the Father," October 1995 general conference, https://www.churchofjesuschrist.org/study/general-conference/1995/10/swallowed-up-in-the-will-of-the-father?lang=eng.

our bodies, what words we say, what goals we set, what kind of people we are, and what kind of people we become. A step deeper into our soul than our choices, our desires reveal who we are at our core. If you are waking up consistently unhappy with the life rising up around you, it may be that your desires are to blame.

Good news: you are in charge of your desires. You may not choose which desires spring up in your heart (just like the gardener can't choose which weeds or bugs come into her garden box), but you can choose which ones grow and which ones are uprooted and cast away.

This process of nourishing, grooming, and weeding our desires is an essential step in leading a purposeful life. President Joseph F. Smith, expert desire gardener, taught that the "education . . . of our desires is one of far-reaching importance to our happiness in life."[2] The primary reason this is true is that what you desire is what you get. This is what Alma marvels about to his preaching pals after they return from teaching the Lamanites—God will give each man what he desires "whether it be unto death or unto life."[3] So when the Jews didn't want to understand Jesus's teachings, He made His teachings hard to understand.[4] When the Nephites didn't want God as their guide, He stopped guiding them.[5] When the people in Bountiful wanted Jesus to stay, He lingered longer.[6] Jesus explains this desire-karma principle

---

2. The Church of Jesus Christ of Latter-day Saints, *Teachings of the Presidents of the Church: Joseph F. Smith* (Salt Lake City: The Church of Jesus Christ of Latter-day Saints, 2011), https://www.churchofjesuschrist.org/study/manual/teachings-joseph-f-smith/chapter-33?lang=eng.
3. Alma 29:4: "I know that he granteth unto men according to their desire, whether it be unto death or unto life."
4. Jacob 4:14: "But behold, the Jews were a stiffnecked people; and they despised the words of plainness, and killed the prophets, and sought for things that they could not understand. Wherefore, because of their blindness, which blindness came by looking beyond the mark, they must needs fall; for God hath taken away his plainness from them, and delivered unto them many things which they cannot understand, because they desired it. And because they desired it God hath done it, that they may stumble."
5. Helaman 12:6: "Behold, they do not desire that the Lord their God, who hath created them, should rule and reign over them; notwithstanding his great goodness and his mercy towards them, they do set at naught his counsels, and they will not that he should be their guide."
6. 3 Nephi 17:5–8.

pretty simply: "Ask and ye shall receive, seek and ye shall find, knock and it shall be opened unto you."[7] As we know, these desires may not be granted immediately, but they will be granted. This is the point that Corianton's dad railed into him after he started pursuing some non-life-giving desires. Modern-day translation: "Whoa, son! You better watch it, cuz what you're going after, you're gonna git."[8]

When President Oaks' mother worried about him making poor decisions, she taught him to "pray about [his] feelings" so that he could know which desires would lead him to good destinations.[9] The power of prayer will also work for you. You can pray to have desires to believe something.[10] You can pray to align your desires with God's desires.[11] You can pray to enjoy something you don't like doing but know you should.[12] After all, if your heart isn't in it, doing the good thing "profiteth you nothing."[13]

While preparing for my fourth or fifth birthday, I accidentally stumbled upon the secret for sifting through life-giving desires and life-destroying desires. It was the day of my party, and I was planning out what I would wish for when I blew out my birthday candles. Should I wish for a pony? A puppy? Maybe a million dollars? (You don't have to be around long to know it's go big or go home when it comes to wishes.) But then I had an absurdly mature thought for a child my age: "The real reason I would want those things is to be happy. So, the best thing to wish for is to be happy." I felt that I had stumbled upon the secret of best wishes to wish for. What good would

---

7. 3 Nephi 14:7: "Ask, and it shall be given unto you; seek, and ye shall find; knock, and it shall be opened unto you."
8. Alma 42:28.
9. Dallin H. Oaks, "The Desires of Our Hearts," BYU devotional address, October 8, 1985, https://speeches.byu.edu/talks/dallin-h-oaks/desires-hearts/.
10. Alma 32.
11. As Jesus prayed in Gethsemane, "Father, if thou be willing, remove this cup from me: nevertheless not my will, but thine, be done" (Luke 22: 42; see Bible Dictionary, "Prayer," The Church of Jesus Christ of Latter-day Saints, https://www.churchofjesuschrist.org/study/scriptures/bd/prayer?lang=eng).
12. 3 Nephi 19: 24: "They did still continue, without ceasing, to pray unto him; and they did not multiply many words, for it was given unto them what they should pray, and they were filled with desire."
13. Moroni 7:9.

a pony or a million dollars be if you weren't happy? You would be a frustrated person cleaning up horse poop or paying an exorbitant amount of taxes. It's not the things we want but rather the result, so cut to the chase and wish for the result itself.

The same secret formula applies to our desires. Often we get focused on wanting the *thing* when really what we want is the *result*. If we first answered the "Where do I want to end up?" question, we'd spend a lot less time sifting through telestial products while looking for celestial results.

Now would be a good time to take a self-examination and ask yourself, "What do I desire most?" As you answer these questions, separate your likes (ice cream) and hobbies (rock climbing) from end results (independence, financial security, living a meaningful life, being significant to someone other than my mirror). Do some soul searching. Take some time to evaluate your desires and decide which desires are going to get you to your end goal and which ones aren't. You will probably find that a lot of your actions (eating ice cream whenever you have a craving) do not align with your true desires (having a strong and healthy body).

Here are some questions to help you identify the desires that currently run your life:

- Who do you look up to and why?
- If you could change one thing about yourself and your life in this moment, what would it be?
- What motivates you to post on social media?
- What about your life will make you proud when you're 103?
- What about your life will make you feel regret when you're 103?
- When do you feel really envious of other people?
- How do you fill your downtime?
- What do you hope heaven is like?
- When you look in the mirror, what do you hope to see?

If going through this exercise helps you realize that many of your desires are focused on temporal or selfish things, change them now! Your desires affect your final destination, and following superficial, worldly desires that don't align with your divine identity will unavoidably leave you feeling lonely, anxious, and never good enough.

Aspire Higher

The unexamined life is not worth living.[1]

—SOCRATES; DIE-HARD FAN OF LIVING LIFE ON PURPOSE

Confessions of a writing teacher here. Out of all the things that drive me crazy in the teaching world, from bad tech days to grading homework on Friday nights, the one thing I absolutely cannot stand is when students hand me their papers and ask, "Is this good?" I've grown to dread this question so much, in fact, that on the first day of class I emphatically ban my students from asking it and then write said ban in capital letters in the middle of the syllabus, not because I expect anyone to actually read the syllabus, but because I will then have something to point to as I look at them in speechless horror when they inevitably ask me *it* during the semester. I can't be too harsh on them, however, because this was my go-to question when I was seeking feedback in school. It's an irresistible question, and I understand its appeal, but it's one we all need to remove from our vocabulary.

When we ask, "Is this good?" whether it's about a school paper, work project, or family chore, we automatically limit the kind of answer we will receive—a yes or a no—and we stifle the quality and quantity of feedback that eager, holistic mentors are itching to give us. In student language, "Is this good?" most often translates to, "Will this get an A?" Spoiler here: Your teachers do not care if you get an A. Trust me. It's not what gets us up in the morning. Instead, we want you to become a master of whatever we are teaching. So ditch the

---

1. Thomas G. West, *Plato's Apology of Socrates: An Interpretation, with a New Translation* (Cornell University Press), https://www.sjsu.edu/people/james.lindahl/courses/Phil70A/s3/apology.pdf.

short-sighted questions. Replacing "Is this good?" with "How can I make this better?" solicits advice that will help take your current endeavor from good to great.

Sometimes I wonder if our Heavenly Parents feel just as frustrated with our limited mindsets and lack of vision regarding our time on earth. Yes, we need to get jobs, marry, make some babies, and do other basic earth-life stuff, but are we as driven to improve ourselves as They are? Or are we like most students out there and more focused on reaching an arbitrary standard than on transforming into new creatures?

Let's say you accept our Parents' challenge and decide to not merely spend your life checking off boxes but really up your game and try to transform yourself. As you start on that path and begin to comprehend the gap between who you are now and who you can become, you will likely experience one of three emotions:

- Apathy (Meh, whatever.)
- Hopelessness (Woe is me!)
- Motivation (I got this!)

You don't have to be a rocket scientist to guess where those first two feelings come from. Be-Miserable-Like-Me Man is very cunning at lulling God's children into a pit of mediocrity. His tactics at spreading apathy, for example, may vary here and there, but they all lead you to the same result—sideline living. Even the ancient Greeks realized how deadly indifference can be to human progress. They believed that every man and woman was born with a divine gift straight from Mt. Olympus—thumos—a drive to be and do better.[2] If Joe or Jane Ecles

---

2. Greeks were not monolithic in their understanding of thumos. Plato's understanding of thumos was more mild and unisex than others. "A Tradition of Thumos," *Classical Wisdom*, June 23, 2014, https://classicalwisdom.com/culture/traditions/tradition-thumos/. Brett McKay and Kate McKay, "Got Thumos?" *The Art of Manliness*, March 11, 2013, last updated June 6, 2021, https://www.artofmanliness.com/articles/got-thumos/. In the thirteenth century, French Philosopher started the counter-cultural movement of the dispassionate life. It has stuck around in American culture as the cool way to live. Most philosophers sense, however, that he got it wrong. When you snub out your will to thrive, you snub out your meaning. Benjamin Storey and Jenna Storey, "Podcast #701: Why Are We Restless?" interview with Brett McKay, *The Art of Manliness*, podcast audio, April 19, 2021, https://www.artofmanliness.com/character/advice/why-are-we-restless/.

was seen loafing around the Panthenon instead of training for the Olympics or writing philosophy, it was because his or her thumos was out of whack and needed a reboot. They knew, just as Joseph Smith taught thousands of years later, that God did not make you to sit around enjoying a bag of Doritos while binge watching the most recent Netflix must-see but to be very much "actively engaged in a good cause."[3]

If a numbing of ambition doesn't work to snuff out your drive for divinity, Satan will most likely turn to the debilitating power of hopelessness and try to overwhelm you with the daunting task of changing. First, he'll make you forget that God is just as invested in your growth as you are, causing you to feel weak and alone. Then, he'll remind you over and over again how unworthy you are and of all that bad stuff you've done. This sneaky satanic strategy is what Alma warns his son about after giving him the change-your-life-before-it's-too-late speech. Having experienced the sin-derived depths of despair himself, Alma knew how harmful dwelling on personal weaknesses can be. And so he offered this advice: "Let this trouble you no more; only let your sins trouble you, with that trouble which shall bring you down unto repentance."[4] Allow your sins and weaknesses to drive you *toward* God and teach you what you need to change, rather than trapping you in a perpetual slump of self-loathing.

This connection between self-awareness and personal improvement was one of the many lessons Moses learned while enrolled at Mountain Top High. Only after he learned to reconcile who he was (mere mortal) with who he could become (God's heir) was he able to cut through Satan's lies and become the deliverer of Israel.[5] Understanding your strengths and weaknesses allows God's perfecting plan to work for you. He can't help you as much if you don't know how much you need His help. God has told us that this life is to "see if [we] will do all things whatsoever the Lord [our] God shall

---

3. D&C 58:27.
4. Alma 42:29.
5. Moses 1.

command."[6] But often we forget who the assessment results are for. They surely aren't for omnipotent God. He already knows everything about us—our strengths, weaknesses, desires. Life's test is for *us* to find out "what lack [we] yet,"[7] not the other way around.

When you know what you lack, you know what you need to change. Social scientists have repeatedly found that those who have a strong sense of their strengths and weaknesses are more effective and productive than those who don't.[8] This is why interviewers love the "What's your biggest weakness?" question. What they really want to know is, "Are you self-aware?"

Learning where you're not so awesome can be painful, embarrassing, even traumatizing. I still get nauseous thinking about a time when I received some uncomfortable public feedback. I was on stage wearing my trendy-but-not-too-trendy blouse-blazer combo, giving a dazzling three-minute speech summarizing the research I was conducting for grad school. The hours of practice and preparation had paid off. Every movement, every line, every word came out just as I had planned. I might as well have been on TED; it was that good. The audience erupted with applause as I bowed and left the stage. They loved me. Unfortunately, the judges didn't. The I-am-so-awesome feeling that I'd had leaving the stage quickly vanished when I walked back on thirty minutes later holding the honorable-mention prize instead of the three-hundred-dollar check that was given to the top three winners. The worst part came when the judges made an oral explanation of their choice: "Awards are based on quality of research, not on presentation. We recommend all participants try again next year when their research is more substantial." You didn't need a master's degree to know that they were talking about

---

6. Abraham 3:25.
7. Matthew 19:20.
8. Travis Bradberry and Jean Greaves, *Emotional Intelligence 2.0* (California: TalentSmart, 2009), 37–38, Kindle. "Self-awareness is so important for job performance that 83 percent of people high in self-awareness are top performers, and just 2 percent of bottom performs are high in self-awareness. Why? When you are self-aware you are far more likely to pursue the right opportunities, put your strengths to work and—perhaps more importantly—keep your emotions from holding you back" (38).

me. They might as well have said it straight: I was a phony. All flash, smiles, and dazzle, whose theatrical show tried to compensate for lackluster research with underwhelming results. I cried for a week. Not because I didn't win the prize, but because they were right. After crawling out of my hole of embarrassment, I made sure that the next time I gave a presentation, my message was meaty as well as engaging.

Lucky for us, self-awareness isn't something that only comes in crucial moments of performance. You can develop it and get better at it at any time. Here are a variety of strategies offered by Church leaders and social scientists that you can use to up your self-awareness game:

- Evaluate past situations: What happened? What did I do?[9]
- Ask your Heavenly Parents to show you how They see you.[10]
- Ask often, "What am I doing that I should stop doing?" and "What am I not doing that I should start doing?"[11]
- Notice how your actions affect other people.[12]
- Identify your triggers. What (or who) makes you lose it?[13]
- Think about yourself in third person to provide some objectivity.[14]
- Look for patterns in your behavior. What does this teach you about yourself?[15]
- Ask for feedback. Sometimes other people can answer those questions for us better than we can. Asking God works, too.[16]

---

9. Sheri Dew, *Insights from a Prophet's Life: Russell M. Nelson* (Salt Lake City: Deseret Book, 2019).
10. Michelle D. Craig, "Eyes to See," October 2020 general conference, https://www.churchofjesuschrist.org/study/general-conference/2020/10/14craig?lang=eng.
11. Craig, "Eyes to See."
12. Bradberry and Greaves, *Emotional Intelligence 2.0*.
13. Bradberry and Greaves, *Emotional Intelligence 2.0*.
14. Bradberry and Greaves, *Emotional Intelligence 2.0*.
15. Bradberry and Greaves, *Emotional Intelligence 2.0*.
16. Larry R. Lawrence, "What Lack I Yet?" October 2015 general conference, https://www.churchofjesuschrist.org/study/general-conference/2015/10/what-lack-i-yet?lang=eng.

Don't hesitate to learn from your mistakes; that's why we have them. Remember, it wasn't until Peter failed the ultimate test—denying Christ—that he recognized his fatal flaw: he feared man more than God. Once he understood this about himself, he was able to change. He stood boldly by his testimony of Jesus until the day he died. Self-awareness for the win.

Part 2
Your Sidekick: Going from Good to Great

The Secret Sauce to an Incredibly Smashing Life

Those who hope in the Lord will renew their strength. They will soar on wings like eagles; they will run and not grow weary, they will walk and not be faint.

—ISAIAH 40:31

Harriet was a stay-at-home mom with barely enough time to keep her seven kids fed, clean, and clothed. How did she galvanize a nation to war in the name of morality?

Patrick was young, enslaved, and depressed. How did he become the hero of a foreign country and an international icon?

Louis was emotionally broken, embittered, and lost. How did he become a symbol of courage and hope and later have a movie made about his life?

These three individuals all have something in common that took their lives from *meh* to *Kazam!* Their secret? Jesus Christ.

No matter how many abilities and skills you obtain on your path of personal progress, hooking up to Christ's power is the only way to completely bust through that glass ceiling that holds our mortal selves down. And the best part? He wants to help you. He has volunteered to walk alongside you, assist you, pull you, carry you—do whatever it takes to save you. The only thing He asks is that we let Him do it. If a superhero with all the power in the world came to you and asked if he could be your sidekick and help you become an all-powerful god like him, you would hoot and holler, jump up and down, and scream out a mighty, "Heck, yes!" To do otherwise would be ludicrous. Not to mention utterly boring.

Christ's influence in your life is what sunlight is to color. When it's dark outside, how many colors can you see? There's only one answer—none. Everything is black, which is not even really a color, just the absence of color. But, when the sun comes out, how many colors do you see? Christ makes all of the difference. You may be the most exquisite aqua-blue violet that the world has never even seen, but without Christ's light shining on you, all you (and the world) can see is a blah gray.

Consider the three individuals I listed at the beginning of this chapter. Each one of them were pretty average individuals, but when they turned to God and invited Him into their lives, they accomplished amazing things—both of temporal and eternal importance.

Harriet Beecher Stowe was a mother of seven living in southern Maine. She liked to write, but it was hard to find the time between the bread-making and diaper-changing. Stuff was messed up in her world, though, and it really bothered her. In 1850, the United States passed the Fugitive Slave Act, which meant that Black men and women who ran away from the abusive slavery lifestyle could not seek freedom in the North, and whoever helped them would face imprisonment. What her country was doing was wrong and Harriet knew it. But how could she make a difference? Sitting in church one day, a scene came to Harriet of a Black man being beaten to death. She suddenly knew what she had to do. She went home and started to write.[1] During nap times, she wrote. While waiting for bread to rise, she wrote. When *Uncle Tom's Cabin* was published in 1852, it met with immediate success. The stirring novel of Tom and his family in slavery helped open the hearts of the Northerners to the atrocities committed against their Black brothers and sisters in the South. Years later, when Harriet met Abraham Lincoln in the White House during the Civil War, Lincoln purportedly saw her and said, "So this is the little lady who started this great war."[2] Regardless of the personal acclaim she received for the

---

1. Charles Edward Stowe, *Life of Harriet Beecher Stowe Compiled from Her Letters and Journals* (Boston: Houghton, Mifflin and Company, 1890; Project Gutenberg, 2004), 148–149, https://www.gutenberg.org/files/6702/6702-h/6702-h.htm.
2. Kimberly J. Largent, "Harriet Beecher Stowe: The Little Woman Who Wrote the Book That Started This Great War," The Ohio State University, accessed October 13, 2021, https://ehistory.osu.edu/articles/harriet-beecher-stowe-little-woman-who-wrote-book-started-great-war.

book, she unfailing gave credit to God. "I did not write that book," she would reply. "The Lord did."³

Now let's turn to the depressed teenager, Saint Patrick. No, he was not a leprechaun. Patrick grew up in a wealthy English home during the late fourth century A.D. He passed his days in leisure, doing what he wanted when he wanted. Although his parents were Christians, Patrick did not believe in God. "Hogwash," he said. When he was sixteen, he was kidnapped by pirates and dragged from his English home to the dank, grungy, and barbaric land of Ireland and sold into slavery. With no one to turn to for comfort or solace, Patrick turned to God. Slowly he developed a relationship with that once distant and foreign being. After six years of bondage, Patrick was awakened in the night and led by God's hand to a ship that carried him back home to England. Although Patrick was happy to see his family again, he had a new and troubling feeling in his heart. Everything he had was due to God's grace. How could he not extend that gift to others? When he later had a dream of the Irish voices calling out to him for help, he made up his mind to return. No, he didn't have any formal religious training. No, he didn't know if the Irish would even listen to him. In fact, it's likely they would try to kill him like most foreigners who visited their land. But God would help him. To the shock and horror of his family and friends, Patrick returned to Ireland and spent the rest of his days teaching the Irish people the gospel of Jesus Christ.⁴ Today, he has a whole holiday named after him. *Bam.*

Louis Zamperini was an Italian-American living in California, and he could run fast. His dream was to win the gold medal in the Olympics. Those plans dissolved when World War II erupted and he was sent to Hawaii to train as a bombardier. He was captured by the Japanese and held as a POW for two years. The torture and physical and emotional trauma he experienced are unspeakable. He returned to his country a broken, embittered man. Unable to prequalify for the

---

3. Stowe, *Life of Harriet Beecher Stowe*, 156. Different versions of this quote exist. The exact quote from the source above is, "I the author of 'Uncle Tom's Cabin'? No, indeed. The Lord himself wrote it, and I was but the humblest of instruments in his hand. To Him alone should be given all the praise."
4. Philip Freeman, *St. Patrick of Ireland* (New York, NY: Simon & Schuster, 2004).

Olympics, unable to maintain a healthy relationship, unable to live in mental peace, Louis was at rock bottom. That is, until he welcomed Christ into his life. Forgiveness, peace, renewal—bit by bit Louis healed. In 1998 he was able to return to Japan as a torch bearer of the Olympics with only brotherly love in his heart toward the country and people who had treated him so cruelly years earlier.[5] A reporter once asked Louis what would have happened if he had never accepted Christ's message to forgive his tormentors. "I wouldn't have a life. I think I'd be dead," Louis said.[6] Thankfully, Louis didn't die. He partnered with Christ and was able to take his story of trial, tears, and ultimate healing to millions of people all over the world.

Christ has proven over and over again that He will do good on His promise to make you into a power to be reckoned with. Yet, with the explosion of scientific discoveries and advances in modern times, an obsession with human might and strength has made many people wonder why they should bother teaming up with God at all. We have more proof than ever of the amazing feats that man can accomplish. We can build rocket ships, travel to the moon, solve complex problems, stave off death in unbelievable ways. We know that humans can do mind-blowing things without calling on the help of God. For some, this is proof of why they don't need God in their lives. Why go through the hassle when you can do so much on your own? Yet, no matter how competent of a human you are, adding God to the mix will *always* increase your final outcome. Mormon stresses this fact when describing the many Nephite wars with the Nephite-haters. During one such battle, Zerahemnah, yet another Nephite dissenter, rallied up the apparently-have-nothing-better-to-do Lamanites to go to war. Despite having zero armor and inferior weapons, the Lamanites were rocking it on the battlefield: "Never had the Lamanites been known to fight with such exceedingly great strength and courage. . . . They

---

5. Laura Hillenbrand, *Unbroken: A World War II Story of Survival, Resilience, and Redemption* (New York: Random House, 2010).
6. John Meroney, "'World War II Isn't Over': Talking to *Unbroken* Veteran Louis Zamperini," *The Atlantic*, November 11, 2014, https://www.theatlantic.com/politics/archive/2014/11/world-war-ii-isnt-over-talking-to-unbroken-veteran-louis-zamperini/382616/.

did fight like dragons, and many of the Nephites were slain by their hands."[7] The Nephites were so intimidated by the ferocious strength and vigor of the Lamanites that they started to run away. Seeing what was happening, Moroni cut off their retreat and reminded them why they were fighting and who was helping them.

The Nephites stopped and prayed for help. "And in that selfsame hour that they cried unto the Lord for their freedom, the Lamanites began to flee before them."[8]

With humans, strength and ability is finite. *With Christ, there are no limits.* Who wouldn't want that kind of power in their lives?

Christ's power has repeatedly made my life better and more successful in a variety of ways, one of which has been with money. When I was finishing my senior year of high school, I went on the hunt for a high-paying job. I had a part-time job at the mall, but the hours were inconsistent, and the hourly rate wouldn't cover my anticipated expenses even if I did work full time. If I were going to save enough for my first semester of college, I needed help. I paid my tithing, prayed for a miracle, and sent some resumes around town. On a whim, I dropped off a resume at a temp agency my sister had worked with once and sat through a skills test to see if they could find a good fit. It didn't seem promising since most temp jobs wouldn't pay much more than I was making at the mall, and my Microsoft Word skills were pretty lackluster. A week into summer vacation, I got a call from the temp agency. They didn't have any availabilities with their clients, but an in-house secretary position had opened up in their Manassas office. It paid great and was full time for as long as I wanted. Was I interested? Heck, yes! Thank you, sidekick!

No matter what your starting point of awesomeness is, God can make it better. I dare you to give it a try. The first step? Choose Him.

---

7. Alma 43:43–44.
8. Alma 43:48–50.

Choose Already

May your choices reflect
your hopes not your fears.[1]

—NELSON MANDELA;
FORGIVER, LEADER, WORLD CHANGER

Napoletanas. Cobblestone roads. Golden-trimmed palaces. Clean streets and bustling motos. I was twenty years old and loving my out-on-my-own adventure in Madrid, Spain. Minus the exploitation and grand-scale massacres, I felt like a 1500s explorer discovering a new land full of people, food, customs, and ideas unlike anything I had ever known.

Yet, this particular day the world was not as vibrant. I paid no attention to the large Rebajas signs advertising insanely low prices of trendy-yet-horribly-made shoes or the three-foot-long pig legs hanging in the carnicería that usually left me gawking in the window as gruff, hairy-handed men gave me a raised eyebrow. I was busy. Pondering the BIG questions.

"Is He real?"
"Or is He not?"
"Is religion a hoax?"
"Or a godsend?"
"Is right and wrong man-dictated?"
"Or of divine design?"

---

1. Lindsey Jacobson, "Remembering Nelson Mandela on the Anniversary of His Inauguration," *ABC News*, May 9, 2017, https://abcnews.go.com/International/remembering-nelson-mandela-anniversary-inauguration/story?id=47205398.

I had spent the prior evening eating tapas with three sophisticated European men who talked sophisticatedly about sophisticated things in such a nonchalant if-everyone-knew-what-I-knew-they'd-have-all-the-answers sort of way.

Yes, I saw the irony in taking life lessons from anyone in a bar, but I knew that once and for all these were questions that I had to address and really answer for myself. The world is full of people who believe a variety of ideas, religions, or world views. But what did I believe? What ideas would I subscribe to?

For most of my life I had primarily associated with people who thought and lived the way I did. What I thought was bad, they thought was bad. What I thought was good, they thought was good. Now in a more intimate way, I was seeing the many different options available for living and believing. In fact, my dad had recently left the Church on the same grounds—found his truth in man and ideas and walked away from "all that religious nonsense." At least if I decided to change paths, I would have someone else, a crowd really, to journey with.

Like my father, I didn't want to live a lifestyle because it was easy, comfortable, or merely familiar. I wanted to be deliberate about what I chose to believe and what my life would look like. I felt the weight of Joshua's rally cry bear down on my soul: "Choose ye this day whom ye will serve."[2]

Most of us have a similar experience at some point in our lives. Sometimes the moment meets us head on like it did to me, but often it pops up in smaller doses over a period of time. Choosing what to believe in is a huge part of why we are here. Scriptural prophets hammer this point home pretty well:

- **LEHI:** [Men] are free to **choose** liberty and eternal life, through the great Mediator of all men, or to **choose** captivity and death.[3]
- **SAMUEL THE LAMANITE:** Ye are free; ye are permitted to act for yourselves . . . that ye might **choose** life or death.[4]

---

2. Joshua 24:15.
3. 2 Nephi 2: 27.
4. Helaman 14:31.

- **MORMON:** For thus sayeth the scripture: **Choose** ye this day, whom ye will serve.[5]
- **NEPHI:** They yield unto the devil and **choose** works of darkness rather than of light.[6]
- **ISAIAH:** Butter shall he eat, that he may know to refuse the evil, and **choose** the good.[7]
- **CHRIST VIA JOSEPH SMITH:** I was ordained from before the foundation of the world for some good end, or bad, as you may **choose** to call it. Judge ye for yourselves.[8]
- **CHRIST TO MOSES:** And unto thy brethren have I said, and also given commandment, that they should love one another, and that they should **choose** me, their Father.[9]

Believe in God, don't believe in God—it's a choice. We often think that if we just had more information we could *know* if God is real and then make our choice. But we don't have all the information. We don't know, so we keep wallowing in uncertainty while looking around longingly at others in both camps and wondering what they know that we don't. In reality, atheists and believers have the same set of facts before them. But between those facts and their beliefs lies a choice—the choice of how to interpret the data.

This is the trouble Alma and Korihor face during their is-God-real-or-isn't-He argument. Where Alma saw divinely inspired words of scripture, Korihor saw self-interested persons speaking for their own gain. Where Alma saw planets orbiting in a god-inspiring dance, Korihor saw the byproduct of billions of years of convenient coincidence.[10] They were both privy to the same events, artifacts, and information, yet the conclusions they drew from those events, artifacts, and information were complete opposites. Believing God is real and hears your prayers or believing that He is a figment of imagination created

---

5. Alma 30:8.
6. 2 Nephi 26:10.
7. Isaiah 7:15–16.
8. D&C 127:2.
9. Moses 7:33.
10. Alma 30.

by hopeful-yet-needy masses both require you to make a choice based on incomplete knowledge. This is why traditionally those who follow Christ and those who do not are called believers and non-believers rather than the informed and the uninformed.

The ultimate freedom to choose what we believe and how we will live our lives is what makes the choice to follow God and obey Him a power-generating force rather than a debilitating one. This power has allowed individuals to walk on water, move mountains, heal thousands, and, most importantly, be cleansed spiritually. In fact, your choice to believe is really the only thing that you can give God. Although our Heavenly Parents created the bodies that house your will and give you the power to carry out your will, They did not create your will, nor are They responsible for what you desire or what you choose. This is the part of you that existed long before you entered spirit-people phase. Elder Neal A. Maxwell teaches that because our will is the only thing that is really ours to begin with, "It is the only possession that is truly ours to give!"[11] Jesus can't use His transforming powers on us unless we choose Him. Deliberately. Once and for all.

So, choose to believe or not to believe. You have the same available facts to consider as anyone else. What's up to you is the conclusion you are going to bet on. As for me, well, since you're reading this book, you can probably guess with whom I decided to place my bet.

---

11. Maxwell, "Swallowed Up."

Attach to God

Love of God is to our consciousness like a string to a high-flying kite. When the connection is strong, we are free to rise to any height.[1]

—DADI JANKI; INDIAN SPIRITUAL LEADER

Once you choose to team up with Christ, His bump-it-up-a-notch power can fuel your life ever upward. Let's clear up a few misconceptions about how this works. To keep Christ's influence strong in your life, you don't need to pray or read your scriptures every day. You do not need to sit in a church building for two hours every Sunday. You don't even need to go to the temple. To keep the presence of Him in your life, you need to do only one thing—strengthen your attachment to God. All of the "standard activities" are standard because they are excellent ways (in fact, God prescribed ways) of connecting with God, but they only work if you approach them with that objective. Reading your scriptures to check off your 365-day reading chart is not going to get you anywhere; reading to more clearly hear God's voice in your life will.[2]

Building a relationship with God is similar to how you build relationships with other people. Fortunately for me, How Not to Have Any Serious Relationships with Anyone could have been my

---

1. This quote is generally attributed to Dadi Janki, but the original source is unknown.
2. Virginia H. Pearce, "Prayer: A Small and Simple Thing," BYU Women's Conference, April 28, 2011, 8, https://womensconference.ce.byu.edu/sites/womensconference.ce.byu.edu/files/virginia_pearce.pdf. "And so the miracle of prayer doesn't reside in the ability to manipulate situations and events, but in the miracle of creating a relationship with God."

second major in college. What were my strategies? Be non-committal. Don't share your true feelings or thoughts with others; only say what you think they want you to say. Be inconsistent about when and how often you talk to people. Have endless amounts of FOMO (fear of missing out)—check your phone constantly when talking to someone else and always feel uneasy being with the same person or in the same place for too long.

Thanks to these serious skills, I had a slew of raving memories and first dates by the end of my sophomore year but nobody to come home to. I'm not just talking about romance. Even good friends were few and far between. I had failed to establish any strings of attachment between myself and other people. For reasons of simplicity, freedom, flexibility, and independence, I intentionally stayed detached from others, romantic or otherwise.

Marriage and family psychologists have repeatedly acknowledged that attachment is the essence of every relationship. Taking moments throughout a day to check in, connect, and concern yourself with another—be it a friend, parent, or spouse—makes or breaks the relationship.[3] These "collecting rituals" ensure you have ample time to talk, listen, and get to know each other.

Creating a strong attachment to your Heavenly Parents is vital to your spiritual survival here on earth. The development of wild birds adds some insight into the importance of this relationship. Within hours after hatching, a duck will imprint on the first moving object it sees (usually the mom or dad). *Imprinting* means that his brain says, "Hey, follow this thing around and do everything that this thing does, because what this thing is, you are." The duckling will then follow the parent around and mimic feeding, walking, and mating behaviors. If, for some reason, instead of first seeing a member of his species when he pops out of the shell, he sees a human (or a different animal, or even a chirping football), he will follow that object around and try to be like that object even to the point of harming or killing himself in

---

3. John M. Gottman and Nan Silver, *The Seven Principles for Making Marriage Work* (New York: Three Rivers Press, 1999), 47–60. Gordon Neufeld and Gabor Maté, *Hold On to Your Kids: Why Parents Need to Matter More Than Peers* (New York, Ballantine Books, 2014), 20–24.

the process.[4] The point is, attachment matters. *Who are you closest to in your life matters.* The closer you are with God, the better off you will be because you will be more likely to mimic the behaviors that will take you from human child to almighty being.

The following six ways of assessing the strength of your relationship with God are based on attachment theory commonly used in couples and family therapy, and they apply well to your connection to your spiritual parents. As you read each one, ask yourself how well it applies to the relationship you have built with God. You, like me, will likely find places where you can improve your connection with Him.

Senses: You feel, hear, see, or speak with God.

You sense God's presence and know when He is close or far. You feel His arms around you as you pray. You recognize His voice. You spend time with Him in His house or other sacred places.

Sameness: You want to be like Him.

You strive to be like God.[5] You copy His behavior like a new kid trying to be in the cool crowd, talking, walking, eating, dressing like He would.[6] Your sense of self merges with God's to the point that His name becomes a synonym for your name.[7] What God would do, you would do.[8]

---

4. "Human-imprinting in Birds and the Importance of Surrogacy," The Wildlife Center of Virginia, accessed June 29, 2021, https://www.wildlifecenter.org/human-imprinting-birds-and-importance-surrogacy#:~:text=Imprinting%20for%20wild%20birds%20is,adult%2C%20providing%20them%20with%20safety.
5. 3 Nephi 27:27: "What manner of men ought ye be? Even as I am."
6. 3 Nephi 27:21: "For the works that ye have seen me do, that shall ye also do."
7. Mosiah 5:8: "Therefore, I would that ye should take upon you the name of Christ."
   "As we choose to be baptized, we begin to take upon ourselves the name of Jesus Christ and choose to identify ourselves with Him. We pledge to become like Him and develop His attributes" (Dale G. Renlund, "Unwavering Commitment to Jesus Christ," October 2019 general conference, https://www.churchofjesuschrist.org/study/general-conference/2019/10/16renlund?lang=eng).
8. 1 Corinthians 6:19.

Belonging and Loyalty: You wear the "I'm a Child of God" badge with pride.

You recognize you are "His"[9] and you are loyal to that family tie. Because of that belonging, you make big promises to do what He asks when He asks it.[10] As such, you consider yourself part of "His people" and a member of "His fold."

Significance: You know you matter to God.[11]

When you feel lost, you know He will guide you.[12] When you are hurt, you know He will succor you. When you are scared, you know He will comfort you. Why? Because you matter to Him.[13] And you know it.

Emotional Intimacy: You keep God close in your thoughts and heart.

You talk to God a lot and tell Him everything, even the seems-trivial-to-others-but-not-to-you details.[14] Keeping Him close mentally helps you know His opinions, ideas, and thoughts.[15] You feel safe, comforted, and strengthened because of this emotional bond.[16]

---

9. Mosiah 5:15: "That Christ, the Lord God Omnipotent, may seal you his."
10. Mosiah 5:5: "Willing to enter into a covenant . . . to do his will."
11. D&C 18:10: "The worth of souls is great in the sight of God."
12. Luke 15:1–7.
13. 1 John 3:16: "Hereby perceive we the love of God, because he laid down his life for us."
14. Psalms 62:8 (NIV): "Trust in him at all times, you people; pour out your hearts to him, for God is our refuge."
15. Mosiah 5:13: "For how knoweth a man the master . . . who is a stranger unto him and is far from the thoughts and intents of his heart."
16. Philippians 4:13 (NKJV): "I can do all things through Christ who strengthens me."
    D&C 6:36: "Look unto me in every thought; doubt not, fear not."

Being Known: You feel He knows you.

You feel that He knows you, all of you, the real you.[17] You are okay showing Him the ugly, mean, dark places of you[18] because He doesn't just know you, He gets you. You feel comfortable being in His presence just as you are, because you know you don't have to pretend to be something you're not for Him to love you.

So, what's the status? Are you and God best buds, or are your bonds of attachment on the tenuous side? Like any relationship, you can never check off "tight with God" as done. It requires constant investment and deposits over the course of a lifetime. If you are feeling disconnected from God, start increasing the amount of time you spend "connecting" with Him during the day. Make daily commitments to sit and talk with Him.[19] Serve Him. Learn about Him. Ponder His words. And don't get FOMO![20] When it's you and God time, be all in. As you more firmly attach to God,[21] you'll find that your strong connection to heaven gives you the lift to truly soar.

---

17. Moses 1:35: "For they are mine and I know them."
18. 1 Samuel 16:7: "For man looketh on the outward appearance, but the Lord looketh on the heart."
19. The Hebrew word for prayer, *tefilah*, is related to the verb *tofel*, meaning attach, join, or bind together. Prayer is the most effective and efficient way to create and strengthen your relationship with your Heavenly Parents. You can't wear it out. Pray every day, all the time. To learn about different types of prayer and when to use them see the appendix (see Nissan Mindel, "The Meaning of Prayer," Chabad.org, accessed March 23, 2022, https://www.chabad.org/library/article_cdo/aid/682090/jewish/The-Meaning-of-Prayer.htm).
20. 1 Nephi 8:25: "And after they had partaken of the fruit of the tree they did cast their eyes about as if they were ashamed."
21. Matthew 11:29–30: "Take my yoke upon you and learn of me; for I am meek and lowly in heart: and ye shall find rest unto your souls. For my yoke is easy, and my burden is light."

Got SQ?

Everything has beauty,
but not everyone sees it.[1]

—CHINESE PROVERB

In the early 1900s, Dr. Terman[2] made a discovery that would change the world. He could measure how smart people are.[3] With one simple test, he could quickly identify the losers from the winners in every field and industry. Now it would be easy to know who to vote for as president or who to accept into the best schools. Thrilled with the possibilities, Terman shared his work with the U.S. military, who excitedly started sifting through recruits based on IQ scores, and colleges and businesses quickly followed suit.[4]

But, it didn't work. It turns out that IQ is a pretty lousy predictor of success. Those with high IQs who were supposed to solve all the problems were not solving them, nor were they doing a decent job leading the less-intelligent masses. Over and over again, those

---

1. This quote is generally attributed to Confucius, but the source is unverified.
2. Lewis Terman built the Stanford-Binet Intelligence Scales (IQ test) adapted from the Binet IQ test developed earlier. Terman and others like him at that time believed your IQ was a fixed quantity from birth to death (see Shenk, *The Genius in All of Us*, 31).
3. Daphne Martschenko, "IQ Tests Have a Dark, Controversial History—but They're Finally Being Used for Good," *Insider*, October 11, 2017, https://www.businessinsider.com/iq-tests-dark-history-finally-being-used-for-good-2017–10.
4. Shenk, *The Genius in All of Us*, 32.

with just average intelligence outperformed those with high IQs in almost every field.[5]

As scientists groped for missing information, they stumbled onto other forms of intelligence that help people succeed—emotional intelligence, physical coordination, spatial awareness, street smarts.[6] This growing list of abilities have helped us better understand human competence, but they all fall short in capturing one of the biggest variables that often separates those who thrive[7] from those who don't—spiritual intelligence: the ability to recognize and understand spiritual things.

Spiritual intelligence is what Paul goes crazy about when talking to the Corinthians. Every group of people he had thus preached to was only able to think about knowledge with a very narrow lens. The Jews wanted scriptural proof; the Greeks, logical conclusions. Each group was unable to comprehend that different types of knowledge exist and are gained in different ways. Paul challenged his listeners to seek knowledge in a new way—with the Spirit: "What we have received is not the spirit of the world, but the Spirit who is from God, so that we may understand what God has freely given us."[8] Paul warned that if we try to understand spiritual things with the same tools used to understand different fields of knowledge, we will miss the point: "For the natural man receiveth not the things of the Spirit of God: for they are foolishness unto him: neither can he know them, because they are spiritually discerned."[9]

As you increase your attachment with your Heavenly Parents, you will find that your SQ will also increase and, as a result, increase your personal potential for awesomeness. SQ is the difference between those

---

5. Bradberry and Greaves, *Emotional Intelligence 2.0*, 21.
6. Shenk, *The Genius in All of Us*, 13–42. The first two chapters of Shenk's book discuss the hang-ups with trying to define, and even more so measure, intelligence.
7. What do I mean by thrive? That you are better off than you would be without it. SQ helps us in a variety of ways. It's impossible to pigeon-hole its impact into one factor. It could be in academics, in business, in relationships, or in finding inner peace. Bottom line: it's real and we need to start acknowledging its role in a wide variety of pursuits beyond religionousity.
8. 1 Corinthians 2:12 (NIV).
9. 1 Corinthians 2:14.

who understand the spiritual workings of the world and those who don't. The scriptures share a slew of stories that illustrate the leg-up spiritual intelligence provides. Consider these examples: Nathan had the SQ to recognize Jesus was the son of God. The Pharisees didn't. Elisha had the SQ to see the hosts of angels upon the hill and therefore remain calm during the battle. His servant didn't.[10] Nephi had the SQ to ask for and find his own spiritual answers. Laman and Lemuel didn't. The wise men had the SQ to know that the star was a blessing. Herod didn't. The righteous Nephites had the SQ to feel that Samuel spoke the truth. The disbelievers didn't. President Nelson has the SQ to understand how God's laws work in the medical field. Many doctors don't.

I saw the power of SQ flow into an individual's life during my time teaching the gospel in Uruguay. While tracting one day, we met the González family. The wife had incredible spiritual intelligence. She had a personal relationship with God and was able to discern God's hand in her life. However, her husband, Facundo, was pretty close to spiritually illiterate. He was unable to see God's hand in anything, much less in his personal affairs. Regardless, he agreed to read the Book of Mormon and follow up with us later. When we visited the next week, the difference in this man was shocking. Facundo was calm, joyful, and excited about God's work. He described a feeling of peace and understanding concerning the death of his first wife and child that replaced feelings of resentment and pain that had haunted him for years. He prayed and felt that someone was listening and, even more incredible, talking back! A whole world he had never known before suddenly became clear and accessible.

Just like it did for Facundo and other scriptural champions, as your SQ increases, your understanding of God's ways and mysteries will also increase. You'll catch the spiritual nuance in personal stories and see the workings of heaven in the mundane. Miracles won't be once-in-a-lifetime sightings but everyday observations. Where others get frustrated about the messy, broken world we live in, you will see the spiritual glue that holds it all together with meaning and purpose.

---

10. 2 Kings 6.

The spiritual world is invisible to the temporally minded,[11] just as emotional undertones are imperceptible to the calloused and logical reasoning is indecipherable to the irrational. Spiritual, emotional, cognitive, or other types of intelligences may seem to conflict with each other now and then, especially at first. But as you spend time developing each type, you will find that they begin to overlap to the point that they become "a fulness of truth,"[12] catapulting you toward your goal of becoming like God, for "the glory of God is intelligence."[13]

---

11. 1 Corinthians 2:14.
12. D&C 93:26; 88:78–79. I love how President Nelson put it: "Truth is truth! It is not divisible, and any part of it cannot be set aside" (Russel M. Nelson, "Let Your Faith Show," April 2014 general conference, https://www.churchofjesuschrist.org/study/general-conference/2014/04/let-your-faith-show?lang=eng).
13. D&C 93:36.

You Are What You Eat

The art of living well is the art of consistently choosing the best.[1]

—WELL-EDUCATED HEART WITH
MARLENE PETERSON; HEART NURTURER

Weird things start happening to you when you serve a full-time mission. For one, you devour Church content like it's Thanksgiving dinner. And when all you read, watch, and listen to are Church magazines, general conference talks, the Tabernacle Choir, scriptures, and so on, you become a walking church service. Everyday events jar scriptures into your mind. You hum hymns in the shower. You daydream about possible scriptural happenings and get giddy sharing Church folklore with your mission buddies at district meetings. By the time you've been in the field for six months, you realize that the adage *you are what you eat* applies to more than just your physical body.

As you pursue SQ and a secure attachment to your Heavenly Parents, you need to pay attention to what you feed your heart and mind on a holistic basis. Just as a certain diet will lead to a certain body type, a certain intake of content will lead to a certain state of mind. If you feel far from heaven, *are you partaking of heavenly substances?* If you have a hard time thinking of nice things, *are you reading uplifting material?* You might think a little unsavory content here and there won't hurt, but even a small amount of murky content takes up space that

---

1. Marlene Peterson, "WEMH #7 Notebooking," *The Well-educated Mother's Heart*, podcast audio, August 17, 2017, https://www.librariesofhopestore.com/podcasts/wemh-7-notebooking.

would otherwise be filled by light. Of course, you don't need to read or listen to only scriptures and general conference talks. God's light can be found in various fields and human creations. Before sending you to this floating rock, Mother and Father placed within your soul a light to help you identify and cling to other light during your earth-life journey.[2] The more spiritual light you are able to gather within you from around you, the stronger your light detecting ability will become.[3] This spiritual spidey-sense will help you know which things will fill you with goodness and which ones wont, but asking these simple questions can help when in a pinch: Does it motivate you to be a better person? Does it direct your thoughts to heaven? Does it make you feel peaceful or cheerful inside? If it doesn't, then it's probably not worth your time.

Unfortunately in today's world, feeding your heart or mind with quality ingredients that enhance any of your intelligences requires constant vigilance. If we left the menu to "things we stumble upon throughout our day," our insides would fill up on billboard catch phrases and social-media click bait before making it to any meal of substance. Don't let junk take up your mind space. Be proactive. Be ruthless about what you consume. As God told Emma, "Lay aside the things of the world and seek for the things of a better."[4]

A diamond mine of "better things" can be easily found in the arts.[5] Yes, like paintings, music, and poetry.

---

2. Also known as the Light of Christ (see D&C 93:2).
3. D&C 50:24: "That which is of God is light; and he that receiveth light, and continueth in God, receiveth more light; and that light groweth brighter and brighter until the perfect day." D&C 88:40: "Light cleaveth unto light."
4. D&C 25:10.
5. Spending time in nature also falls in this category. You can't get away from the fact that something spiritual resides in the very bones of the woods. Almost every human culture has connected nature with God's hand in some way. German artists in nineteenth century at the height of the romantic period understood this connection. As one connoisseur put it, "Nature was considered to be the visible spirit, the evidence of the divine in the absence of an image of God himself. The romantic landscape artist was charged with the responsibility of contemplating nature and its spirit and then replicating it in art" (Kira Gurmail-Kaufmann, "7 Things You Need to Know About German Romanticism," *Sotheby's*, November 29, 2018, https://www.sothebys.com/en/articles/7–things-you-need-to-know-about-german-romanticism).

No! Please don't close the book!

Stay with me on this one. I promise it'll be worth your time.

The arts, especially fine art, are swept under the rug these days as frivolous and cryptic and too niche to be accessible to you and me. But if we have patience to study them, they can keep the heart mellow and malleable. Music,[6] stories, art, and poetry capture layers of meaning. On the surface they are sounds in the air, paint on a canvas, or words on a page, but when masterfully arranged, these simple elements communicate something far more powerful and profound. Their inherent elusiveness harnesses the power of the spirit to carry meaning into the heart through symbols. Although we live in a world where we primarily understand our experiences through five physical senses, God teaches that "all things are spiritual."[7] Everything you touch, see, smell, and hear has a spiritual meaning underlying its physical appearance. A study in the arts is a study in the language of the spirit.

I haven't found a stronger example of the spirit-nourishing power of the arts than in the life of Charles Darwin. As a boy, Darwin was extremely sensitive to right and wrong—especially regarding the treatment of animals. Growing up in mid-1800 England, horses were

---

6. Greek and Chinese cultures (500 B.C.–A.D. 300) saw a link between what music one listens to and what kind of person you are. For that reason, listening to uplifting music was an ethical choice rather than an aesthetic one (Yuhwen Wang, "The Ethical Power of Music: Ancient Greek and Chinese Thoughts," *Journal of Aesthetic Education* 38, no. 1 [2004]: 89–104, accessed March 24, 2021, doi:10.2307/3527365). Translation from an ancient Chinese text quoted in Wang, "The Ethical Power of Music," 90: "Men have powers of the body and powers of the mind but they can not remain stable with regard to grief, pleasure, joy, and anger. They are moved by external causes. Thus originates the appearance of the various affections. Therefore, if feeble, trivial, and rushed music prevails, people will be sad. If harmonious, peaceful, varied but simple music prevails, people will be gratified and happy. If vigorous, violent, and forceful music prevails, which arouses people to move their limbs and animates their blood circulation, they will be steadfast and resolute. If straightforward, steady, peaceful, and stately music prevails, people will be dignified and pious. If broad, serene, orderly, and flowing music prevails, people will be compassionate. If licentious, evil, hasty, and superficial music prevails, people will be dissolute."
7. D&C 29:34.

commonly overworked as taxis, and bears were forced to fight with dogs for entertainment. It was actually this cruelty that first made him question the existence of God.[8] As his journey continued, he had many experiences where he felt the influence of the Spirit in his life. On his first journey to South America as a young man, he describes the wide variety of terrains, from the luscious jungles of the Amazon to the rocky expanse of Tierra de Fuego: "Both are temples filled with the varied productions of the God of Nature:—no one can stand in these solicitudes unmoved, and not feel that there is more in man than the mere breath of his body."[9]

Regardless of a few moments of recognition of a Supreme Power, Darwin never found clarity when it came to religion or man's relationship to God.[10] His wife, Emma Wedgwood, a strong and devout Christian, advised him that if he spent as much time nourishing his heart as he did nourishing his mind, he would find the answers that troubled his soul.[11] Later on in his life, he attributed his lack of spiritual adeptness to his neglect of art, music, poetry, and other subjects that soften the heart to influences of the Spirit: "If I had to live my life again, I would have made a rule to read some poetry and listen to some music at least once every week; for perhaps the parts of my brain now atrophied would thus have been kept active through use. The loss of these tastes is a loss of happiness, and may possibly be injurious to the intellect, and more probably to the moral character, by enfeebling the emotional part of our nature."[12]

Interestingly, Albert Einstein, who nourished a lifelong love of the arts, especially music and poetry, was able to maintain a belief

---

8. James D. Loy and Kent M. Loy, *Emma Darwin: a Victorian Life* (Gainesville, FL: University Press of Florida, 2010), 308.
Slavery and other inhumane acts that man did to man also caused him to doubt the existence of God (S. Michael Wilcox, *10 Great Souls I Want to Meet in Heaven* [Salt Lake City, UT: Deseret Book, 2012], 154).
9. Charles Darwin, The Voyage of the Beagle (New York: New American Library, 1988), Internet Archive, 436, https://archive.org/details/voyageofbeagleme00char/page/436/mode/2up.
10. Loy and Loy, *Emma Darwin,* 309.
11. Loy and Loy, *Emma Darwin,* 84–85.
12. Nora Barlow, ed., *The Autobiography of Charles Darwin* (New York, NY: W.W. Norton & Company, Inc., 1958), 139.

in a Supreme Creator throughout his scientific career. Although he never affiliated with a church and did not believe in a personal God, Einstein was able to intertwine the existence of divinity with scientific discoveries. In fact, after validating the field of quantum mechanics, Einstein spent the last half of his life trying to find a way to disprove the fundamental beliefs of the field that implied the universe is random, unpredictable, and devoid of purpose. His main reason for believing that his contemporaries' findings were false? "A feeling" that "deep down it is wrong, even if it is empirically and logically right."[13]

Having a strong spiritual intelligence allows you to see and understand the world as God does. It's worth any spiritual-food diet you need to go on. For a short but blessed time of my life, I would go to the gym at the outrageous hour of 5:30 a.m. where, alongside twenty other women, I would lift weights under the tutelage of the strongest, fittest woman I had ever laid eyes on. She was ripped, hot, peppy, and built like a rock. We did what she told us to do because of the compelling proof of product right before our eyes. While we were struggling under our barbells completing the umpteenth chest press, she would lecture on the importance of eating nutrient-rich food during the day. "You can't build a brick house with marshmallows. If you want to build a brick house, you need to eat bricks." The same goes for your spiritual health. *You can't build a celestial testimony if you're only intaking telestial materials.*

It's time to toss the spiritual junk food. Be picky about what you consume. Don't watch trash. Don't read trash. Don't do trash. Seriously consider the quality of the shows you watch, especially those that you consume on a regular basis. Sometimes the pre-selected ratings of shows and movies are helpful in making these decisions, but often you have to set your own standards for what is worth your time and what is not. This goes for music, social media posts, books, and web articles. Learn how to value your mind space to the point that content has to pass a high threshold of quality for you to spend your precious time on it. Apply this rule of thumb: If

---

13. Walter Isaacson, *Einstein: His Life and Universe* (New York: Simon and Schuster, 2008), 345.

it's not a "heck yes," it's a "no."[14] As you become a connoisseur of good rather than a garbage disposal of whatever comes your way, you'll find that your spiritual intelligence will increase as well as your capacity to live a light-filled life.[15, 16]

---

14. This rule of thumb is adapted from Greg McKeown's fabulous read *Essentialism: The Disciplined Pursuit of Less* (New York: Crown Business, 2014).
15. I know what you're thinking: "Where in the world do I find fine art and poetry?" For fine art, going to a museum in the flesh is the best way to pick up on the essence of the creation, but in a pinch digital images work, too. The National Gallery of Art at nga.gov is committed to sharing as many fine art images to the public free of charge as possible. You can see what they are currently showing in their exhibits or use their filters to find works of art from various countries, time periods, or genres. The website simplejoyart.com specializes in images from the late 1800s to the early 1900s and has enough variety for you to picture study to your heart's content. When you look at a work of art, whether digitally or in person, ask these three questions: What does this remind me of? What do I notice? What do I wonder? These help you engage with the creation and bring more purpose to your gaze. (Thanks, Marlene, for this tip! See footnote 1 of this chapter for a link to her podcast.)
16. To get started with poetry reading, here are two collections that I love: *The Best-Loved Poems of Jacqueline Kennedy Onassis*, compiled by Caroline Kennedy. Whether you're a Kennedy fan or not, this is a great selection of poems that are accessible to everyone. There are poems of all kinds—short, long, funny, patriotic, famous, obscure. I suggest that you read slowly. Sometimes I have to read a poem a dozen times before it starts to mean something to me. But honestly, that's the fun of the process—feeling meaning unravel itself with time and thought. *A Child's Garden of Verses*, Robert Louis Stevenson. Robert had a gift for writing all kinds of genres, but his poems, especially the ones for children, never get old. If you are new to the poetry world, I highly recommend checking out his work.

The Ram's Way

With pride, there are many curses.
With humility, there come many blessings.[1]

—EZRA TAFT BENSON; LEADER OF LIGHT

Dead drunk and hopeless. That was how Bill W. felt in 1934 when he found himself hospitalized for the fourth time at Towns Hospital for alcoholism. But this time, Bill realized something that had never occurred to him before—he could not stop drinking. He couldn't do it. He was an alcoholic, and the urge to drink was stronger than his will or ability to ignore it. Ironically, it was this realization that saved him. After accepting the extent of his helplessness, Bill cried out to God for help.[2] Bill never touched a bottle after that day. He went on to write a book about his experience and the principles that he felt would help other alcoholics, specifically about the need to accept your inability to stop drinking and to turn to a higher power for help.[3] Since that time, millions of people have followed Bill's path to sobriety by applying the Twelve Steps that he and his cofounder helped develop. The organization they started, Alcoholics Anonymous, continues to help millions of people overcome addiction today.

---

1. Ezra Taft Benson, "Cleansing the Inner Vessel," April 1986 general conference, https://www.churchofjesuschrist.org/study/general-conference/1986/04/cleansing-the-inner-vessel?lang=eng.
2. Alcoholics Anonymous World Services, *'Pass It On': The Story of Bill Wilson and How the A. A. Message Reached the World* (New York: Alcoholics Anonymous World Services, Inc., 1984).
3. "Bill's Story," *Stepping Stones*, accessed October 15, 2021, https://www.steppingstones.org/about/the-wilsons/bills-story/.

It sounds like a no-brainer to lean on God and make Him your sidekick, but often it's not until people hit rock bottom, like our pal Bill, that they finally give up trying to do it on their own and let God help them. But why? If it's so easy and comes with such obvious benefits, why don't more people do it? Well, for really one reason—the P-word. Yes, P as in pride. The same force that kept Laman from untying Nephi even as the large waves threatened to crush him and his family. The same force that stalled Naaman from bathing in the river seven times to heal his leprosy. The same force that kept Nicodemus from leaving his pharisee post and following the Son of God. Pride shows itself in many forms, but its impact is singular—to draw you away from heavenly aid.

Consider these four common types of pride:

- **Receive and Forget:** God teaches us to fly, but once we are in the air, we rapidly forget who helped us get up there in the first place.
- **Thanks, but No Thanks**: The ego—the appeal of doing something all by yourself because *you* don't need help. Or the close imposter—thinking you are too unworthy to deserve help. That's pride disguised as humility. Don't be fooled, pride works both ways, thinking you are better *or* worse than you really are. True humility is letting God define your identity, not the other way around.
- **Prove It:** Out of all the types of pride, demanding to be convinced has got to be the most frustrating one for our Heavenly Parents. They've already boomed this planet together out of the sky, featured it with resources to meet all of our many needs, packaged our spirit in a body, plus who knows what else, and now, like a spoiled six-year-old who doesn't think the pony present is good enough, we demand more. We won't accept help until They prove X, Y, or Z. It's not like all They're asking is to let Them save us from spiritual and physical death while making us into super gods in the process or anything. Geez.
- **Yeah, but:** You've received a sign or knowledge or light or whatever, but something is holding you back from taking

God's promise seriously. This type of pride, commonly known as doubt, is similar to a black hole. When matter approaches a black hole, the pull of the hole elongates objects as they get closer—stretching them out and making them appear larger than they really are. Then the hole continues to grow and suck everything within its proximity into nothingness. Doubt behaves in a similar way. It skews concerns or problems so that they appear larger than they really are and, if left unchecked, doubt continues to expand until even the things you knew for sure get consumed by it.

All four types of pride seek to separate you from God's power. Recognizing that you can't do it alone and asking for God's help is the surest path to obtain endless strength. Rams and other horned animals are a beautiful symbol of this spiritual phenomenon. Since a ram's horns are on the top of its head, it can only utilize the horns' power and protection by lowering its head. If instead the ram tried to raise its head while fighting, it would reveal the weakest and most vulnerable part of its body—the jugular vein—and risk certain death.[4] Just like the ram, it is impossible for us to release all of our promised *spiritual power* if we do not bow our heads in humility and allow God to help us.

To the godless, power derived from humility is incomprehensible. Consider the Lamanite leader Zerahemnah who, despite having an army twice as large, was defeated big-time by Captain Moroni's meager crew. Moroni told Zerahemnah that they had won thanks to God's protection; but Zerahemnah refused to believe it. "No, no," he said. "You won because your armor and your brains are better. A god had nothing to do with it."[5]

Unbelievers don't understand how heaven's aid works, and they will try to attribute your victory, strength, success, and so on to something else. Something tangible and temporal, such as genes, money, grit,

---

4. I heard the symbol of the ram in a BYU devotional by Terence Vinson ("Meekly Placing Our Total Trust in God," BYU devotional address, February 11, 2020, https://speeches.byu.edu/talks/terence-m-vinson/meekly-placing-our-total-trust-in-god/).
5. Alma 44:9.

or dumb luck. Don't fall for it. You know who helped you succeed. Denying God's hand in your life is the losers' way. If anyone out there could claim self-success, it would be Christ, but even He repeatedly passed on credit for His accomplishments to His Father.

Now, *please* don't confuse the fourth type of pride (doubt) with seeking understanding. They are totally different. Questions are honest desires to seek truth—whatever the answer may be—with the intention to move forward. Doubt is spiritual paralysis. Instead of propelling your search forward, it brings it to a standstill. While seekers walk forward with humility, doubters hide behind justification. The biggest way to tell the difference between seeking and doubting is how it feels. I learned to feel this difference from one of the ugliest men I have ever met.

His name was Diego. And as I said, this guy was challenged in the good looks department. He had deep-set eyes and black coarse hair, and his back stooped when he walked. In more ways than one he resembled a live version of Quasimodo from *The Hunchback of Notre Dame*. And like Quasimodo, his spirit was as gentle as his face was fierce. I first met Diego while knocking doors with my missionary companion in the small town of Fray Bentos. We initially met his mother, but while she wanted nothing to do with us, Diego was intrigued. We left him with a Book of Mormon and returned a few days later to check up on his interest and progress. In our rather routine missionary way, we looked him in the eyes and asked directly, "Do you believe that the Book of Mormon is true?"

His eyes met our gaze. Then, without hesitation or the slightest sign of wavering, he replied simply, "Who am I to doubt the word of God?"

JAW DROP.

What?

No one had ever answered like that before. Ever. I had never even accepted my own spiritual promptings with such guileless faith.

His simple, humble response was heart-breakingly powerful and heart-meltingly gentle at the same time. In that instant, I became painfully aware that so many of my doubts, skepticisms, and cynicisms are bred in the mire of pride. Pride to reject. Pride to challenge. Pride to think I am owed more than I have been given.

Over the years, I have thought many times about Diego and his simple example of faith. It has convinced me that humility is the only light that can bring you through the darkness of doubt and into the patient pursuit of seeking answers.

Another way to check yourself from setting up shop in the streets of skepticism is to strengthen your stance on the things you do know. Elder Lawrence Corbridge shared his experience with this in the extreme. His assignment as a member of the Seventy was to read anti-Mormon literature,[6] which, in spiritual terms, is akin to camping in the den of the dark arts. Do you remember how interacting with Voldemort at close distance sapped Harry's physical strength and emotional stamina? Or how the faces of the sith lords in *Star Wars* started to erode the longer they worked for the dark side? Or how wearing the ring-to-rule-them-all around his neck became heavy and painful for Frodo during his journey? Evil takes a toll on you. The lies and powers of Satan weigh heavy in our hearts and minds and make us feel depressed, anxious, frustrated, and angry. For this reason, cyber-security squads who look for bad guys in the dark corners of the World Wide Web have to take frequent mental health breaks just to maintain their emotional well-being and stave off overwhelming feelings of despair.[7]

But back to Corbridge. He would leave work depressed and exhausted after wading through a relentless swamp of negative and critical material. The only way he could keep from submitting to the tumultuous attack of the Mormon haters was to relentlessly and frequently remind himself of the truths he did know. God lives. Jesus is our Savior. Joseph Smith was a prophet. The Book of Mormon is true. He called these the "answers to the primary questions." If you know the answers to these questions, very little depends on your ability to answer questions such as, "Where is the sword of Laban?" "Why

---

6. Lawrence E. Corbridge, "Stand Forever," BYU devotional address, January 22, 2019, https://speeches.byu.edu/talks/lawrence-e-corbridge/stand-for-ever/.
7. Conor Pope, "Inside the Dark Web: The Truth Is There Is a Lot of Evil Out There," IrishTimes.com, October 13, 2018, https://www.irishtimes.com/culture/tv-radio-web/inside-the-dark-web-the-truth-is-there-is-a-lot-of-evil-out-there-1.3653092. Deb Radcliff, "Protecting the Mental Health of Cyber Warriors," Sans.org, October 30, 2019, https://www.sans.org/blog/protecting-the-mental-health-of-cyber-warriors/.

don't women have the priesthood?" or "Will polygamy be a thing in heaven?" Once we find answers to the primary questions, we can wait confidently for the secondary questions to be answered, knowing that God's promises are true—that He loves us and that we cannot even imagine the "things God has prepared for them that love Him."[8]

Humility is a source of power. Breathe it in deep and keep it with you. Like Bill, it can be the secret to overcoming your challenges. Like Diego and Corbridge, it will fill your life with truth and light. When you come up against a tide of despair and discouragement, hold tight to what you do know. Be humble and believe.[9]

---

8. 1 Corinthians 2:9.
9. Mosiah 4:9 "Believe in God; believe that he is, and that he created all things, both in heaven and in earth; believe that he has all wisdom, and all power, both in heaven and in earth; believe that man doth not comprehend all the things which the Lord can comprehend."

I Choose to Live *Here*

Your life is a result of the
choices you have made.
If you don't like your life,
start making better choices.[1]

—ZIG ZIGLAR;
HUSBAND, FATHER, BELIEVER, MOTIVATOR

In the 1800s, one word held extreme popularity among politicians, journalists, novelists, and regular Janes and Joes, but since that time, that word has nearly lost usage.[2] What is that word? Virtue. And no, not virtue as in sexual purity. That's what our day has watered down virtue to mean. Virtue as in power and strength. Specifically inner power and strength obtained by constantly seeking and internalizing the good.

At least one thought leader in past civilizations has taught that moral virtue is necessary for true greatness.[3] Confucius taught that

---

1. Zig Ziglar, "Your life is a result of the choices you have made. If you don't like your life, start making better choices," Facebook, December 8, 2013, https://www.facebook.com/ZigZiglar/posts/10152064931912863:0.
2. Google Books Ngram Viewer, https://books.google.com/ngrams/graph?content=virtue&year_start=1800&year_end=2019&corpus=26&smoothing=3&direct_url=t1%3B%2Cvirtue%3B%2Cc0.
3. C. S. Lewis, *The Abolition of Man* in *The Complete C. S. Lewis Signature Classics* (New York: HarperCollins, 2002), 691–704. Lewis studied the moral codes of various civilizations extensively. He argued that the similarities of moral codes in human societies across time and space proved the existence of objective moral laws. I find it interesting that so many thought leaders believed that "being good" was essential to living what we would call an abundant life.

virtue in the individual would lead to happy families, stable communities, and prosperous kingdoms.[4] Ancient Hinduism believed virtue to be an inherent characteristic of divinity.[5] Aristotle considered virtue necessary for avoiding self-destruction.[6] Egyptian goddess Maat stressed that virtuous living ensured joy in the afterlife.[7]

Thanks to Christ's teachings, we know how to obtain virtue and its associated power—obey His commandments.[8] Choosing which commandments or moral laws we obey determines in a large sense what kind of world we experience here on earth.

Take Sally and Lucy, for example. Sally's life is filled with jerks and idiots. Someone is always out to get her in one way or another. Last week it was the nosey neighbor who doesn't know how to mind her own business. This week it's her boss who can't recognize brilliance when it dances in front of his nose. Sally barely squeaks by with a C average in school even with cheating, which she wouldn't have to do if her teachers graded fairly and didn't favor the rich kids. Despite having a large group of peers to hang out with at school, Sally often gets bored and frustrated at how self-centered and shallow everyone

---

4. Confucious, *The Great Learning* (The Internet Classics Archive, ca 500 B.C.E.), accessed October 15, 2020, http://classics.mit.edu/Confucius/learning.html. "The ancients who wished to illustrate illustrious virtue throughout the kingdom, first ordered well their own states. Wishing to order well their states, they first regulated their families. Wishing to regulate their families, they first cultivated their persons. Wishing to cultivate their persons, they first rectified their hearts. Wishing to rectify their hearts, they first sought to be sincere in their thoughts. Wishing to be sincere in their thoughts, they first extended to the utmost their knowledge. Such extension of knowledge lay in the investigation of things."
5. Lewis, *The Abolition of Man*, 700–701.
6. Aristotle, *Nicomachaen Ethics,* trans. W.D. Ross, (The Internet Classics Archive, 350 B.C.E.), accessed July 17, 2021, http://classics.mit.edu/Aristotle/nicomachaen.html.
7. James P. Allen, *Middle Egyptian: An Introduction to the Language and Culture of Hieroglyphs,* 2nd ed. (Cambridge: Cambridge University Press, 2010) 119–121. Denise Martin, "Maat and Order in African Cosmology: A Conceptual Tool for Understanding Indigenous Knowledge," *Journal of Black Studies* 38, no. 6 (2008): 951–67, accessed July 18, 2021, http://www.jstor.org/stable/40035033.
8. 1 John 3:22,24; 1 John 4:12–13; Celestial glory resides within us as we keep the commandments.

is. She knows that if she lived in a cooler place with cooler friends, her problems would be solved.

Then there's Lucy. Lucy works at the same place as Sally, lives in the same neighborhood, goes to the same school, and has a lot of the same friends. Yet, she might as well live on a different planet. Lucy has never met a mean person in her life. She sees everyone as a friend, or at least a fellow traveler on the same journey. Lucy doesn't excel at school either, but she doesn't cheat because she wants to give herself the chance to struggle and grow. She frequently has deep, intimate conversations with her friends and awes at how unique and yet similar each person is. She wakes up each day excited to see what adventures life will surprise her with at any moment.

We've all known a Sally or a Lucy in our life. Chances are we've been both a Sally and a Lucy at some point. And like them, the degree to which you enjoy your short time on this spinning orb of dust depends a lot on what rules you choose to follow. The scriptures teach us that there are degrees of heaven called kingdoms and that each kingdom subscribes to different rules or laws. The higher the law we live, the more of God's light enters into our hearts. The more light within us, the happier we are.[9] When we reject to live God's highest laws, less light is able to reside within us, drastically hindering our ability to experience existence in its fullest.[10]

Alma says that at the last days, those who have acquired more light within them will be restored to that same degree of light, while those who have acquired darkness within them will be restored to

---

9. D&C 50:24: "That which is of God is light; and he that receiveth light, and continueth in God, receiveth more light; and that light groweth brighter and brighter until the perfect day."
10. Isaiah 8:20: "To the law and to the testimony; and if they speak not according to this word, it is because there is no light in them. And they shall pass through it, hardly bestead and hungry: and it shall come to pass, that when they shall be hungry, they shall fret themselves, and curse their king and their God, and look upward. And they shall look unto the earth; and behold trouble and darkness, dimness of anguish; and they shall be driven to darkness." Mosiah 2:37, 41.
John 10:10: "I am come that they might have life, and that they might have it more abundantly."

darkness.[11] The word *restore* means to "put back," and something can only be put back that was there in the first place. Although being surrounded by celestial light in heaven will be, well, heavenly, it may not feel all that different from living with the internal light we've filled our hearts with while on earth. Alma does call Judgment Day a day of restoration, *not* a day of promotion.

If this is true, we need to change how we traditionally think about good behavior. Somewhere along the way, Western religion has propagated the belief that good behavior is the price we pay to receive the endurance reward at life's finish line. *"Don't be bad, Johnny; God's watching."* But good behavior is not the price; it's the reward. We don't need to tell the truth to get into heaven. Heaven is telling the truth. We don't need to be chaste to get into heaven. Heaven is being chaste. We don't need to serve others to get into heaven. Heaven is serving others. Rather than how to get into heaven, Christ teaches us how to *become* heaven.[12]

With this in mind, it will matter little if the different kingdoms of heaven are in fact separate physical locations or just different states of being. C. S. Lewis, the spiritual metaphor master, captures this situation beautifully in *The Last Battle*, the final book in his Narnia series. At the end of the world, several followers of Aslan (the Christ figure) enter into his kingdom. To their surprise they see a group of wicked dwarves there, too. The dwarves are sitting by themselves, shivering and complaining about being hungry. Wanting to help them, one of Aslan's followers asks Aslan to get the dwarves some food or warm blankets.

---

11. Alma 41:3–4, 10, 14–15.
12. Many tend to think of the various kingdoms of glory as physical places. If you are in the terrestrial kingdom, for example, the kingdom is surrounded by a wall prohibiting you from leaving and visiting higher kingdoms. That could be. But it may be that we will all be physically with each other but emotionally, spiritually, intellectually, and mentally in different places. In *The Discovery of Joy*, Richard Eyre presents a unique, in-depth look into what joy is, why we crave it, and how to obtain it. Spoiler: joy is not a monolithic emotion. Instead, we experience different types of joy derived from different types of experiences. I believe we experience the highest form of joy when we are living God's highest laws.

"Sure," says Aslan.

He blows his magic lion breath and, voilà! A fancy four-course meal appears paired with golden goblets of the best wine. The dwarves hungrily reach for the food but almost immediately spit it out and complain, "Yuck, this tastes like garbage!"

"Dirty trough water, again. Why don't we ever get anything decent to eat around here?"

Instead of fine silverware and decadent delights, the dwarves are only able to see and taste moldy bread and rotten food. Their own internal misery projects onto their external situation, regardless of their physical location.[13]

As we become more virtuous, our ability to fill our life with miracles will also increase. Enzio Bushe learned to live on a higher plane and in turn fill his life with godly power.[14] Bushe became a member of the Church in his early thirties in post-World War II Germany. Through trial and error, he learned to harness the Spirit in his life and live the commandments with complete trust in God's promises. As he did so, his life was full of miracles—from heavenly help at his business to a healing spirit in his home to an inner transformation resulting in lasting peace, meekness, and joy. He made things happen in his life that most of us only dream about.[15]

When I first learned about Bushe and his miracle-filled life, I couldn't help but wonder, "Why am I not having miracles happen in *my* life? Why did Bushe feel peace when he was financially broke but I only feel frustrated and forsaken? How did he have time to serve his neighbors, build chapels, and help the missionaries when I don't even have time to pray for my ministering sisters? Why am I living in despair while he journeyed along in peace and thanksgiving?"

---

13. C. S. Lewis, *The Last Battle* (New York: Macmillan, 1956; Project Gutenberg Canada, 2014), chapter 13, https://gutenberg.ca/ebooks/lewiscs-lastbattle/lewiscs-lastbattle-00–h.html.
14. Jan Underwood Pinborough, "Elder F. Enzio Busche: To the Ends of the Earth," *Ensign*, February 1985, https://www.churchofjesuschrist.org/study/ensign/1985/02/elder-f-enzio-busche-to-the-ends-of-the-earth?lang=eng.
15. F. Enzio Busche, *Yearning for the Living God: Reflections from the Life of F. Enzio Busche*, compiled by Tracie A. Lamb, (Salt Lake City: Deseret Book, 2004).

You know where I'm going with this. Bushe and I were living such different lives because I wasn't playing by the same rules he was playing by. I wasn't seeking virtue; I was seeking success. I wasn't obeying the highest laws; I was obeying the me-first laws. Daily miracles and a constant flow of God's power in our lives does not need to be the exception; it can be the norm for anyone who takes it up a notch and accepts God's invitation to seek and internalize the good.

The characteristics below describe people who live life on a lower plane followed by a group of phrases that describe people who live life more fully and abundantly. Which words describe you? (Note: These lists are not exhaustive. I've left empty lines so that you can fill in some characteristics that you've noticed.)

Those who live in a lower plane of life and experience life's joys to a lesser degree are those who

- lie to avoid looking bad
- place material success as highest ambition
- hurt other people, either physically or emotionally
- resent people who succeed
- break promises
- avoid thinking for self and instead merely do whatever other people say they should do
- worship what they want rather than what deserves their worship
- complain
- complete chosen tasks half-heartedly
- worry
- gossip
- watch, read, or listen to junk
- belittle
- live passively
- spread rumors without validating their sources
- troll
- avoid looking stupid or vulnerable at all costs
- sloth around
- waste money
- ghost people

- make excuses for failing or bad choices
- think they're better than other people
- brag about how awesome they are
- hold grudges
- compare themselves to others
- want to please other people at all costs
- throw pity parties
- use people for their own pleasure/needs
- speak the truth to put others down
- do what they want when they want regardless of others' needs
- live to consume and entertain self
- blame others for mistakes
- hide their true feelings and beliefs due to shame
- don't care for their physical bodies (whether that's not exercising, overeating, under eating, self-abuse, not self-grooming)
- beautify their bodies as a way to feel superior or better than others
- smirk, roll eyes, or scoff
- make choices out of fear
- _____
- _____
- _____
- _____
- _____
- _____

Those who live life on a higher plane and experience heaven while on earth are those who
- help out quickly and often
- tell the truth even if it makes them look bad
- say nice things to and about other people
- make and keep commitments
- work hard
- persist in doing good
- repent

- are humble
- ask for help
- pray
- give respect where it's due
- show reverence to sacred things
- take action
- assume responsibility for mistakes
- forgive quickly
- respect their bodies and actively care for them
- beautify their bodies as a way to honor their creator
- go the extra mile in their work
- prioritize helping others
- share their spiritual knowledge with love
- take personal honesty and integrity seriously
- respect others' feelings and bodies
- speak the truth to build others up
- prioritize service and worship to God
- fulfill personal duties
- smile
- find joy in the day-to-day
- enjoy nature
- listen sincerely to what other people have to say
- _____
- _____
- _____
- _____
- _____
- _____
- _____

What plane are you living on? What's holding you back from living the life of power and action, peace, and light that Christ offers? What can you do today to live differently?

We are gods-in-training, not gods. You don't have the ability to live on the higher plane 100 percent of the time. So when you slip, it's not because you're a loser. It's because you're mortal. Even Jesus didn't consider Himself perfect until He was resurrected.[16] You will have bad days. You will get cut off while driving, you will be treated rudely by clerks at the grocery store, you will stub your toe, and you will lose it. But being aware that you are largely in charge of what you are experiencing can help reel you in when your choices start to drag your life into the mud.

Thanks to Christ's guidance and His super sidekick power, we can experience heaven-like living while on earth.[17] Living these higher laws is hard, but He will help us. As we aim to become more virtuous—more filled with light and good—more joy and power will fill our mortal journey.

I am motivated to live my life on a higher plane due to the times I have experienced the warm-fuzzies of celestial living vicariously through the virtuous lives of other people. I'll always remember the older married couple who taught me this. It was Mormon day at the local ski resort in Northern Pennsylvania, and my youth group stopped at their house on our way out of town. I had never met this couple before; I knew very little about them. But you walked into their home and WHAM! Good feelings hit you in the doorway. Their home was seeping with peace and calmness. It was intoxicating. At first I thought it was the cheesy grandma decorating, or perhaps the jars of potpourri along the banister. Yet as I observed their behavior during our stay, I realized it felt so good in their home because *they* were so good. Over the years I've found other homes and met other people around the world who have confirmed this conclusion. Be good and enjoy the good feelings of goodness.

---

16. This point was introduced to me in Jane Clayson Johnson's book *Silent Souls Weeping*. I don't know why I had never realized that fact before! Before His death, Jesus says, "Be thou perfect even as my Father in heaven is perfect." After His death and resurrection, He says, "Be thou perfect even as I and my Father are perfect." It also helps to remember that perfect in this context means whole and complete, not simply "doesn't make mistakes." A narrow view of being perfect leaves you feeling hopeless, not hopeful (see Jane Clayson Johnson, Silent Souls Weeping: *Depression—Sharing Stories, Finding Hope* [Salt Lake City: Deseret Book, 2018], 53, Kindle.
17. Mosiah 2:41.

Part 3
The Hard Thing about Hard Things

Broken Pieces

Healing does not mean the damage never existed.
It means the damage no longer controls our lives.[1]

—AKSHAY DUBEY;
MOUNTAIN CLIMBER, EXPLORER, LIFTER

If your dad dies while you are in the womb, you are at greater risk for cavities by age two.[2] If your parents divorce during your adolescence, you're likely to get lower grades in school.[3] If you are neglected as a child, you'll probably end up in needy or emotionally distanced relationships.[4] If you are an ethnic minority, you are at higher risk for type 2 diabetes.[5]

Sometimes it seems we don't stand a chance of making it out of here in one piece, let alone as a capable, functioning, thriving being.

---

1. Although widely attributed to Dubey, the original source of this quote is unknown (Akshay Dubey, "Healing doesn't mean the damage never existed. It means the damage no longer controls your life . . ." Goodreads, accessed October 19, 2021, https://www.goodreads.com/author/quotes/7046878.Akshay_Dubey).
2. Elizabeth Noble and Leo Sorger, *Having Twins and More: A Parent's Guide to Multiple Pregnancy, Birth, and Early Childhood*, 3rd ed. (New York; Houghton Mifflin Company, 2003), 120.
3. Jane Anderson, "The Impact of Family Structure on the Health of Children: Effects of Divorce," *The Linacre quarterly* vol. 81,4 (2014): 378–87. doi:10.1179/0024363914Z.00000000087.
4. Sharon Begley, *Train Your Mind, Change Your Brain: How a New Science Reveals Our Extraordinary Potential to Transforms Ourselves* (New York: Ballantine Books, 2008), 187–190.
5. Kimberly Goad, "What's Race Got to Do with Diabetes?" AARP, November 2, 2018, https://www.aarp.org/health/healthy-living/info-2018/role-of-race-in-diabetes.html#:~:text=African%20Americans%2C%20Hispanics%2C%20American%20Indians,American%20Diabetes%20Association%20(ADA).

Besides the consequences of our own inevitable poor choices, a million factors outside of our control pose serious negative effects on our lives. Taking that bleak reality into account, a guest psychologist on a podcast I recently listened to advised those who have gone through trauma or abuse to accept that they are "damaged goods" because some things cannot be undone.[6]

Thankfully, I know that is a lie.

Yes, we can be really, really scarred and damaged by life's experiences. These damages can reverberate through time and generations—often being passed down from broken parent to soon-to-be broken child. But permanent damage is not the message of the gospel. All of our scars and broken pieces can be healed. All of our pains can be alleviated.

Christ's healing power is so central to the universe's existence that we take its power for granted all the time. Consider the shadows of this amazing power in our natural world:

- Spring comes after winter.
- Skin heals when it's cut.
- Lizards grow back lost tails.
- Forests emerge green and healthy after devastating fires.

Can you imagine the first time one of Adam and Eve's kids broke an arm while chasing a saber-toothed tiger up a tree? She probably freaked out and worried about how she was going to survive with a throbbing appendage hanging useless at her side. I can just imagine her surprise when she woke up one day and realized that her broken arm was no longer broken. No doubt, she threw herself to the ground in prayer and thanked God for the unexpected, yet life-changing miracle.[7]

---

6. Joseph Burgo, "Podcast #509: Good Shame; Bad Shame," interview with Brett McKay, *The Art of Manliness*, podcast audio, May 20, 2019, https://www.artofmanliness.com/articles/shame/.

7. We've developed casts to optimize the healing process. Without a cast, maybe our ancestors got weirdly mended bones. Whatever the result, they were probably still amazed it healed at all.

What Adam and Eve's kids saw as a godsend, we consider nothing special. Not only do we expect bones to heal after they break, but we also know how they do it. Yet, does understanding *how* the hematoma and callus stitch the broken bone back together make the fact that it *does* any less amazing? Or any less of a manifestation of our Parents' love for us?

Understanding the opportunities for temporal healing here on earth can fuel our faith that complete, eternal healing is possible in the Resurrection. Even now, researchers in many fields are uncovering more and more amazing ways that our bodies heal—physically and emotionally—in this life. For centuries, most serious scientists believed that certain physical injuries were beyond repair, particularly when it came to the brain. Once a person passed the "critical period" for development, learning, growth, and healing were considered impossible. This was why in 1959, when Pedro Bach-y-Rita suffered a severe stroke, doctors refused to offer more than the obligatory four weeks of rehab and advised his family to put him in an institution. Thankfully, Pedro's son George didn't realize how scientifically hopeless his dad's case was. He took him home and—with the patience of a parent guiding a young child through the developmental milestones of crawling, walking, and talking—George helped his father regain all his past functioning. One year after his stroke, Pedro was back in New York teaching as a professor at City College.[8]

It turns out the brain is a lot more healable than we thought. Not only does the human brain keep changing after adolescence, but it can also do full-scale renovations, from adding new suites to tearing down complete floors. Thanks to modern studies on neuroplasticity (the brain's power to change), high school dropouts who couldn't get beyond a third-grade reading level are training their brains to overcome learning disabilities. Men and women who were born blind are training their brains to see shadows and shapes with electric currents to their skin.[9]

On the emotional front, leaders in the fields of psychology are rapidly rejecting the Freudian belief that we are victims of our past

---

8. Norman Doidge, *The Brain that Changes Itself: Stories of Personal Triumph from the Frontiers of Brain Science* (New York: Penguin Group, 2007), 20–23.
9. Doidge, *The Brain that Changes Itself*, chapters 2–3.

as the evidence accumulates that healing is possible and survivors can live again. Acceptance and commitment therapy[10] is just one example of how we are learning to overcome our frailties and become stronger from the inside out. In this practice, patients learn to relate to their painful memories in productive ways, how to accept life as a whole (the good and the bad), and how to move forward focused on personal values and priorities. Other studies have found that if you were neglected as a child and as a result struggle to keep healthy intimate relationships, you can reverse those negative effects by focusing on personal or third-person stories of secure attachment.[11]

Here on earth, we receive small teasers of Christ's healing power. Healing from physical sickness doesn't stave off death; it just delays it for a while. Overcoming hate and trauma today does not make us immune from emotional turmoil tomorrow. In our post-earth days, however, we are promised physical and emotional healing that is complete and forever. Considering how good temporary healing feels, what we have coming should be pretty awesome.

But physical and emotional healing are not the only benefits of Christ's Atonement that we get to experience on earth. In the here and now, Christ invites us to be healed spiritually, to wash our souls clean from sin, and to become more godly.[12] It was this type of healing that, in the mid-1700s, turned John Newton's life around. For the previous nine years, John had worked as a captain of a slave trade vessel that bought African slaves off the coast of Sierra Leon and sold them to various British ports around the Atlantic. In an effort to maximize the amount of money per voyage, John and his crew would cram as many prisoners as possible into the boat hull, making them lie on small bunks with hardly any space in between to lift their heads. Slaves were shackled at the wrists and ankles, and many were raped, beaten, or tortured as a way to discourage uprisings. Despite having been held as a slave himself for a number of years, John showed little empathy to

---

10. Steven C. Hayes and Spencer Smith, *Get Out of Your Mind & Into Your Life: The New Acceptance and Commitment Therapy* (Oakland, CA: New Harbinger Publications, Inc, 2005).
11. Begley, *Train Your Mind*, 198–202.
12. i.e., being sanctified.

his passengers. To be great, one had to be rich, and he would make his place in the world at any cost.[13]

If light and truth are the ingredients for peace and happiness, neither of those two emotions had much room in John's heart. He had long ago crowded them out with his hunger for wealth and his disregard for human life.[14] Yet, even John was not beyond the Healer's grasp. In 1774, about to leave on another voyage, John became terribly sick and was forced to leave his post. As he convalesced, John became aware of his spiritual brokenness. No longer able to justify his actions, he walked away from his life as a sea captain, dedicated his life to God, and devoted many of his days fighting for the abolition of the slave trade in England.[15] He went on to describe his spiritual rescue and healing in a poem that later became the lyrics of one of the most recognizable songs in the English-speaking world:

Amazing grace!
How sweet the sound
that saved a wretch like me!
I once was lost,
but now am found.
Was blind but now I see.

---

13. John Newton, *Thoughts Upon the African Slave Trade* (London: Printed for J. Buckland, in Pater-Noster Row; and J. Johnson, in St. Paul's Church-yard, 1788), Internet Archive, https://archive.org/details/thoughtsuponafri00newt/page/n3/mode/2up. "Those who are long conversant with such scenes as these are liable to imbibe a spirit of ferociousness and savage insensibility, of which human nature, depraved as it is, is not, ordinarily capable" (17–18).
14. It's important to note that Newton was already a Christian and maybe even a minister before he quit the slave trade. However, he later acknowledges that he wasn't really a believer at that time and his conversion occurred over many years (see Janet and Geoff Benge, *John Newton: Change of Heart* [Seattle, WA: YWAM Publishing, 2018], 119, 135–136.
15. It was because of the work of William Wilberforce and other abolitionists that John began talking actively about his experiences in the slave trade.

Miracle Emotions

Holding a grudge is like drinking poison and
expecting someone else to die.[1]

—AN OLDIE BUT A GOODIE

Twelve years ago on Christmas Eve, after having just watched the latest *Twilight* movie at the theater with some friends, I gloomily walked home from the train station obsessing over a boy who I wanted to call me but who wasn't. Having just watched Bella and Edward sparkle and dazzle their magic all over the big screen didn't help my needy emotional state, either.

While caught up in the midst of my personal rain cloud, a dark car pulled up a few yards ahead of me and stopped abruptly. A big, burly guy stepped out of the back passenger door and, fuming with anger, walked up to me, grabbed me by the shoulder, and punched me in the left eye, smashing my head against the brick wall of an apartment building. When I crumpled to the ground, he grabbed my shoulder bag and took off. I wasn't super with it, but I do remember getting the last word in and yelling, "You big jerk!" as the car sped down the street. As I convalesced in my lonely apartment with a piece of frozen meat on my face, the fact that someday (two years in fact) the feeling in the left side of my nose would come back, or that someday

---

1. This saying has evolved over time and is not attributed to one particular person. "Resentment Is Like Taking Poison and Waiting for the Other Person to Die," Quote Investigator, August 19, 2017, https://quoteinvestigator.com/2017/08/19/resentment/.

(date still pending) I wouldn't flinch every time I passed a man on the sidewalk, wasn't uber comforting.

Some of the worst pains we face during this mortal sojourn come from the loser choices of other people. And while we fight to get to a place of healing, hate and anger often get in the way. And so we stew.

Still stewing?

Probably. Because sitting in those emotions won't lead you away from them. There is only one thing that will—forgiveness.[2] Elsa from *Frozen* may not have been a convincing sixth spirit, but she said it right the first time: "Let it go."

Hate and anger destroy us from the inside out precisely because these feelings go against our inherent desire to love others.[3] It's like going to bed with a full bladder. When you wake up, your internal organs are throbbing in pain trying to keep in what is supposed to come out. Hate is the pain that originates from trying to hold in the love that is natural and instinctive to our nature. If you are feeling anger or resentment toward someone, you need to work on letting your love for that person come through unobstructed. This is the lesson twenty-year-old Corrie Ten Boom learned when the love of her life dumped her to marry a more wealthy "suitable" girl. She was devastated. Before her pain could consume her, her wise, always insightful father gave her the best advice of her life: "If you want the pain to stop, keep loving him. Not how you used to, but as God does. Ask God to help you love him

---

2. Richard G. Scott, "Healing the Tragic Scars of Abuse," April 1992 general conference, https://www.churchofjesuschrist.org/study/general-conference/1992/04/healing-the-tragic-scars-of-abuse?lang=eng. "Forgiveness heals terrible, tragic wounds, for it allows the love of God to purge your heart and mind of the poison of hate. It cleanses your consciousness of the desire for revenge. It makes place for the purifying, healing, restoring love of the Lord."
3. Giving place for our inherent desire to be good and charitable is the principal message in *The Anatomy of Peace*. Although it presents itself as a business self-help book, it does a fantastic job of exploring our inherent sense of goodness and how staying true to that legacy is the only and surest way to inner peace. (The Arbinger Institute, *The Anatomy of Peace: Resolving the Heart of Conflict* [San Francisco, CA: Berrett-Koehler Publishers, Inc., 2006]).

as He loves him."[4] It was this lesson that later saved Corrie again from the consuming flames of hatred when faced with the choice to forgive the men and women who betrayed, imprisoned, and tormented her and other members of her family in German-occupied Europe during World War II leading to the death of her father, sister, brother, and nephew. In what could have become a barrier to her living a joy-filled life, Corrie instead asked for God's help in forgiving her persecutors, allowing her to live and love uninhibited.[5]

In a godless world, this type of healing after trauma or tragedy would be impossible. But not only can God help us find peace after horrific experiences, He can also help us become stronger than we were before. Only recently have psychologists clued into the growth-accelerating power of pain and suffering. After studying hundreds of individuals who had experienced some sort of trauma in their lives—from the death of a loved one, to abuse, to being a POW, to surviving a natural disaster, to you name it—researchers found this surprising quirk: More than half of the survivors identified at least one positive change in their lives due to the experienced trauma,[6] while fewer than 15 percent of survivors developed psychiatric disorders such as PTSD.[7] Not only were people rebounding after experiencing trauma, but many were coming off stronger than before. Researchers even came up with a scientific term for what they were seeing: post-traumatic growth.

---

4. Corrie Ten Boom, John Sherrill, and Elizabeth Sherrill, *The Hiding Place* (New Jersey: Chosen Books, 1971), 47.
This is a paraphrase. The direct quote is, "Corrie, do you know what hurts so very much? It's love. Love is the strongest force in the world, and when it is blocked that means pain. There are two things we can do when this happens. We can kill the love so that it stops hurting. But then of course part of us dies, too. Or, Corrie, we can ask God to open up another route for that love to travel, . . . if you ask Him, He will give you His love for this man, a love nothing can prevent, nothing destroy. Whenever we cannot love in the old, human way, Corrie, God can give us the perfect way."
5. Corrie Ten Boom, John Sherrill, and Elizabeth Sherrill, *The Hiding Place* (New Jersey: Chosen Books, 1971), 215.
6. Richard G. Tedeschi and Lawrence G. Calhoun, "Posttraumatic Growth: Conceptual Foundations and Empirical Evidence," *Psychological Inquiry* 15 no.1 (2004): 1–18, https://doi.org/10.1207/s15327965pli1501_01.
7. Sheryl Sandberg and Adam Grant, *Option B: Facing Adversity, Building Resilience, and Finding Joy* (New York: Alfred A. Knopf, 2017), 164–165.

This emotional growth after trauma is in large part a choice. Not that anyone can choose to skip out on the grief or pain—that unfortunately comes as a packaged deal—but you do get to choose how you will change in response to what has happened to you. I witnessed two experiences with death that taught me this lesson.

While my companion and I were tracting in a rural town in Uruguay, we knocked on the door of a yellow house that sat alone at the end of a street. A disheveled woman in her fifties cracked open the door. Behind her on the sofa lay a framed picture of a young woman. Plastic flowers of pink and blue lay strewn around the room with other memorabilia. When the woman saw our religious tags, she burst into tears. Her granddaughter had been killed in a car accident the year before. As she talked, it was clear that the pain she felt was just as fresh as it had been the day of the wreck. But she was not interested in Christ's message. Anger, bitterness, and grief were stronger than her desire to find peace or healing at that time. She closed the door and continued to sob.

A few years later, I witnessed another family handle the tragic loss of a loved one. Christina had lived a few doors down from me during my elementary to middle school years. We had roamed the neighborhood together with our gang of friends, and our adventures had been frequent and diverse—from playing princess in Christina's unfinished basement to making forts out of the scrap concrete and metal in the abandoned lot next door. Life had been largely carefree, and my childhood was pretty close to perfect. I moved away the year we all started high school. Christina and I saw each other once or twice over the next decade, but besides social media, we were largely out of touch.

While skimming my Facebook feed a few years after my mission, I read that Christina had passed away. She'd had a rare form of cancer that she'd been fighting for years. As I searched her Facebook page, I stumbled upon a set of family pictures Christina and her family had taken months earlier. It was obvious from the information they had posted about her illness that they had all known at the time the pictures were taken that they didn't have much time left together. And yet, they were smiling. Their smiles weren't feigned. They didn't even seem sad. How could this be?

A year later I moved back to the area and decided to visit Christina's family. I knocked nervously at the door.

Will they recognize me? Will they think it's weird I'm here? Is it too soon to visit?

Soon, the door opened and Christina's mother, Amy, let me in. The living room was redecorated, and the kitchen had been updated, but it all felt familiar. I was overwhelmed by the love and peace that was palpable in their home. Although it was obvious that Amy missed Christina, she was not consumed by grief. Love and hope radiated from her face as we talked about some of my childhood memories playing at their home. Somehow I knew without her saying it—Christina's death had brought their family closer to God and transformed their home, even just fleetingly, to a heaven on earth.[8]

Once we recognize the possibilities for growth and positive change in even our darkest hours, we open ourselves up to feel a surprising emotion—gratitude. Gratitude is merely seeing the world how God sees it. When God created the light and the darkness, He saw that it was good. When He created the earth and the sea, He saw that it was good. When He created man and woman, He saw that it was good. The little made-by-God stamp infuses His creations with a shining, beautiful gold aura. Seeing God's thumbprint in our lives requires that we remember our true relationship with God and Jesus, how we really got here, and the real purpose for this mortal existence. Gratitude isn't about changing our perspective of reality. It's about *accepting* reality. The mortal-life-is-the-best-thing-that-has-ever-happened-to-my-existence-thus-far-no-matter-how-seemingly-boring-lame-or-even-tragic-a-life-I'm-living reality.

Accepting reality also helps us fight the gratitude-busting feelings of entitlement that we often experience immediately following tragic upsets. When we get comfortable with life, we start to expect that comfort and ease should be the norm. In fact, when things don't go that way, we feel cheated, let down, and betrayed. We end up

---

8. I believe that Christina's family was able to feel these positive feelings in times of grief because of the higher laws they were choosing to live such as hope, faith, humility, selflessness, and patience. We can all access these types of blessings if we choose to live on a higher plane.

shaking our fists up at heaven shouting, "Why me?" Elder D. Todd Christofferson says "a belief that the world or some other person, government or entity is responsible for meeting your needs and ensuring your comfort and happiness is deadening."[9]

The same spiritual numbing happens when we put that requirement on God. Fighting feelings of entitlement can be hard because often we receive a constant flow of good things that come at little personal effort. If anything, experiences that jar us from our lulled state of ease and tranquility can help remind us how good we normally have it. Chances are that if you are feeling embittered toward life or God, you need to recalibrate your expectations and ask, "Is this really something I am owed or just something I have been taking for granted?"

Seeing life as God sees it (life, whatever it is, is good) can be the secret to succeeding at something versus floundering under the weight of a difficult task. If you want to see the magic of how this works, look no further than the god-fearing, austere-dressing, self-government trendsetting Pilgrims. Almost immediately after arriving at the blessed rock of the promised land, they suffered. Within three months, half of their company had died from starvation and disease.[10] Yet, even on their death beds they persisted in praising and thanking their God. The captain and crew who had brought them over to America mocked their guileless faith.[11]

"Bah, you're all delusional. God does not love you!"

But when the crew began to fall ill, they suddenly saw that the Pilgrims' persistent gratitude gave them something the crew didn't have—inner peace. While the sailors lay dying, they cursed their families, friends, and foes. While the Pilgrims lay dying, they thanked the Good Lord for His grace and mercy. Their circumstances were

---

9. D. Todd Christofferson, "Gratitude, Responsibility, and Faith," BYU–Idaho Commencement Address, December 21, 2018, https://video.byui.edu/media/Elder+D.+Todd+Christofferson+-+%E2%80%9CGratitude,++Responsibility,+and+Faith%E2%80%9D/1_qc354wqh/84734132.
10. William Bradford, "Of Plymouth Plantation," in *The Norton Anthology of American Literature*, ed. Julia Reidhead (New York: Norton & Company, Inc., 2007), 121.
11. Bradford, "Of Plymouth Plantation," 122.

the same. For many, their outcome was the same. But how they experienced it was totally different.

In the face of hardship, peace in the place of anger or angst is one of the greatest miracles the power of forgiveness and gratitude can add to your life.

The Depths of Despair

I'm FINE: Freaked out, Insecure,
Neurotic, and Emotional.[1]

—THE ITALIAN JOB

los·er /ˈlo͞ozər/ n. Someone who sucks at life and should just give up already. Synonyms: Susie McGann.

If that's not what's listed in the dictionary, it should be. At least that would reflect the number of times my loser status has seemed like a reality to me. I've faced some hard things in my life, but the hardest have not been trauma, money problems, or bodily handicaps, but the battle of my own mind. Feelings of darkness, doubt, and fear have immobilized me in the depths of despair for weeks, if not months or longer. Apparently, I'm not alone. Feelings of loneliness, failure, worthlessness, and self-harm are increasing—and fast. Most teenagers and young adults will feel the grips of depression and other mental illnesses at least once within a five-year span. In Utah, suicide is the leading cause of death among fifteen- to twenty-four-year-olds.[2]

Visualizations, positive affirmations, solid belief in self and god genes aside, you can't expect to go about rocking this life when your mental health is floundering. It's like trying to drive a car when the

---

1. Tom Davis, "Italian Job—What 'fine' stands for," YouTube video, 0:39, March 17, 2010, https://www.youtube.com/watch?v=KfcrM7ukzCU.
2. "Health Indicator Report of Suicide," Utah Department of Health, January 5, 2021, https://ibis.health.utah.gov/ibisph-view/indicator/view/SuicDth.AgeSex.html.

steering wheel is broken. No matter how hard you tug, the wheels are not going to budge.

Traditionally we've thought of mental health as either you have it or you don't, but psychologists now understand mental health and mental illness to be more like a mercury-filled thermometer. Sometimes it's high, sometimes it's low, and sometimes we languish in the middle.[3] As researchers have spent more time studying the mind, the more they agree on one thing—it's a beast. Your mind is the crossroads of every aspect of your existence—biological, physical, social, mental, spiritual, and many more -als. That means a poor diet and lack of sleep can negatively impact your mental health. But a yummy salad and meaningful, intimate relationships can boost your mental health.

While we're only at the beginning of understanding the mind, researchers do know that the ill brain is biologically different from the healthy brain. When you have depression, for example, your reward systems are off.[4] Doing fun things do not seem fun. In fact, you are incapable of registering fun activities as fun. It's not a bad-attitude thing; it's a my-brain-is-not-working-right thing.

A crushing part about mental illness is that often its symptoms are the same as sin. When we sin, the Spirit leaves and we lose the beautiful fruits of its presence: joy, love, peace, happiness. But when we have a mental disease, we often feel the same way.[5]

All of us live in sin, so looking for ways to increase your alignment to God's laws will never be a bad idea. But while the negative consequences of sin motivate you to make changes in your life, mental

---

3. Adam Grant, "There's a Name for the Blah You're Feeling: It's Called Languishing," *The New York Times*, April 19, 2021, https://www.nytimes.com/2021/04/19/well/mind/covid-mental-health-languishing.html.
4. Seraphina Seow, "Feel Like You Don't Enjoy Anything Anymore? There's a Name for That—and You Can Break Through It," *Real Simple*, November 18, 2020, https://www.realsimple.com/health/mind-mood/anhedonia.
5. Johnson shares a lot of personal stories of members of the Church who experienced these feelings while suffering from mental illness. (See Johnson, *Silent Souls Weeping*.) Mental illnesses come in all shapes and sizes. I focus mostly on depression in this section because that has been my personal experience, but there are many other types.

illness leads to opposite behaviors. It inhibits action, lowers motivation, and traps you in darkness. If you are facing feelings of hopelessness and despair that do not dissipate and you feel like you are in a hole that you cannot crawl out of, you're battling a mental problem and you need help.

The most common thing people do when their mental health is floundering, or they are experiencing a mental disorder, is nothing. Well, nothing constructive. Self-hate, worry, anger, embarrassment, and denial are some of the emotions we allow ourselves to sit in, unable to move forward. In more than ten different countries over the span of multiple years, researchers found that 45 to 82 percent of people suffering from a mental illness never seek help.[6] And if they do, they wait eleven years on average before doing so.[7] That's a lot of people suffering longer and harder than they need to. You don't need to spend hours and months and years hating yourself or others because your brain is not functioning. That just keeps you out of the game, and that's exactly what Lame Brother wants you to do. Don't fall for it. Managing your mental health is an important part of you taking control of your life. It's not a "maybe I should look for help" thing; it's an "I want to do whatever I can to increase my potential and so I'm going to continuously find ways to optimize my mental health as much as possible" thing.

If you are struggling in the mental department, seeking help, no matter if you end up with a diagnosis or not, is a good thing. Counselors and therapists are trained to help you better understand what you are feeling and experiencing and will always have something you can do to strengthen your mental fitness. It can be hard to put money into something so intangible as mental health, but it's worth the investment. You wouldn't consider putting up with a broken arm just to save on medical bills. Why do that with your mind, which is vastly more essential to your well-being? Speaking to a professional or

---

6. "Mental Health Has Bigger Challenges Than Stigma," Mental Health Million Project 2021, Sapien Labs, https://mentalstateoftheworld.report/wp-content/uploads/2021/05/Rapid-Report-2021–Help-Seeking.pdf.
7. "Mental Health by the Numbers," National Alliance on Mental Illness, last updated March 2021, https://www.nami.org/mhstats.

visiting sites such as OK2TALK.org, where people anonymously talk about what they are feeling, will help you find the vocabulary and phrases to describe how you feel. That in and of itself can be freeing. And while you can bet on picking up some haters who are going to scoff, laugh, belittle, or unfriend you when you start actively tackling your mental health issues, ignore them. They get to choose how they handle their problems; you are choosing to take control of yours.

Besides seeing a counselor, you can do a lot of things to keep your mental health strong, regardless of whether you have a mental illness or not. In 2003, Amy Morin, a recent graduate starting a psychotherapist career, found herself dealing with a mental health battle when her mother died unexpectedly of a brain aneurism.[8] Three years later, on the anniversary of her mother's death, her husband died suddenly of a heart attack. At twenty-six, when most of her friends were enjoying many of life's beginnings, Amy found herself at too many endings. The stress, grief, loneliness, and other my-life-is-over feelings were impeding her from going to work and functioning as a human. Because of her psychology background, she realized that if she wanted to thrive (or even survive) she needed to stop doing certain behaviors before they dragged her down into a deeper pit of mental dysfunction.[9] She wrote a list of Things Mentally Strong People Don't Do as a reminder of what behaviors to stay away from. She has since shared her lists with millions of others around the world and has become a global leader on maintaining mental strength.[10] The following don'ts are recommendations compiled from her lists and from other psychotherapists. What are some behaviors you can change to keep yourself in the mentally-healthy-and-strong zone?

---

8. Colby Itkowitz, "The Sudden Back-To-Back Deaths of Her Mother and Husband Taught Her 13 Ways Not to Grieve," *The Washington Post*, October 15, 2015, https://www.washingtonpost.com/news/inspired-life/wp/2015/10/15/the-sudden-back-to-back-deaths-of-her-mother-and-husband-taught-her-how-not-to-grieve/.
9. Itkowitz, "13 Ways Not to Grieve."
10. "About," Amy Morin, LSCW, accessed July 27, 2021, https://amymorinlcsw.com/about-amy/.

1. **Don't neglect relationships.** Just feeling connected to others can help you maintain a strong mind. Don't take these connections for granted! Deposit daily in family and friend relationships—give 'em a call, send a positive text, remember birthdays. Nurturing relationships will help keep you feeling loved and create a strong support system you can lean on when you go through personal challenges.[11]

2. **Don't forget to help others.** There's a reason service is such a core message of Jesus's gospel—helping other people keeps your mind healthy and happy.[12] I had a friend who found herself sitting at home one day feeling sorry for herself. Realizing that what she was doing wasn't helping her feel better, she instead got up, made cookies, and brought some over. Not only did that make my day, but it also helped her shift her focus away from her problems, strengthen a friendship, and feel God's love. I've tried this strategy in my own life, and it works!

3. **Don't hide your emotions.** You don't have to blast your social media feeds with your current emotional update, but it's important to share how you feel, *really feel*, with others, preferably people you are close to. Just talking about your problems, without seeking any solution or aid, can help you move past inhibiting emotions or thoughts.[13] If you don't have someone to talk to, writing your feelings down can often have the same effect.[14]

4. **Don't skimp on sleep.** Sleep deprivation is the leading mental health issue among college students![15] If you want to feel unable to handle life, sleep as little as possible.

5. **Don't binge to feel better.** As a Latter-day Saint, you may not turn to alcohol or drugs to forget about your problems, but what about that quart of ice cream in the freezer? Gorging on

---

11. Ross Szabo and Melanie Hall, *Behind Happy Faces: Taking Charge of Your Mental Health, a Guide for Young Adults* (California, Volt Press, 2007), 58.
12. Johnson, *Silent Souls Weeping*, chapter 2.
13. Szabo and Hall, *Behind Happy Faces*, 29.
14. "Journaling for Mental Health," *Health Encyclopedia*, The University of Rochester Medical Center, accessed July 27, 2021, https://www.urmc.rochester.edu/encyclopedia/content.aspx?ContentID=4552&ContentTypeID=1.
15. Szabo and Hall, *Behind Happy Faces*, 24.

junk food or other harmful substances may alleviate your pain temporarily, but when the effect wears off, you'll feel worse than you did before.[16]

6. **Don't stay in bed in the fetal position.** This is my go-to when I am dealing with low mental health. Why get out of bed when you feel like *blah*? Moving your body can change the chemical balance in your brain, boosting your "happy hormones."[17] Even just standing in a power pose with your arms and legs spread wide and your chest open can trick your brain into feeling awesome.[18] Try it.

7. **Don't insist on being perfect.** Perfectionism is often a symptom of low self-esteem. You seek praise and attention to feel valued; if you are not the best, others won't notice you, or worse, they'll see your flaws.[19] Be okay with being seen—your strengths *and* weaknesses. This humble confidence will give you power to be okay with failure while still striving for excellence—at a doable pace.

8. **Don't dwell on the past.**[20] It happened. And luckily for you, you have the gospel perspective to realize that whatever occurred in the past matters little to nil in your eternal future. Let yourself move on.

9. **Don't resent other people's success.**[21] I'm guilty of this one, too. It's so easy to feel like a loser when everyone else seems to be rocking it and you aren't. But good vibes beget good vibes. Set

---

16. "How to Look After Your Mental Health," Mental Health Foundation, accessed July 27, 2021, https://www.mentalhealth.org.uk/publications/how-to-mental-health.
17. "Depression and Anxiety: Exercise Eases Symptoms," Mayo Clinic, September 27, 2017, https://www.mayoclinic.org/diseases-conditions/depression/in-depth/depression-and-exercise/art-20046495.
18. Amy Cuddy, *Presence: Bringing Your Boldest Self to Your Biggest Challenges* (New York: Little, Brown Spark, 2015), chapter 6, ebook.
19. Amy Morin, *13 Things Mentally Strong Women Don't Do: Own Your Power, Channel Your Confidence, and Find Your Authentic Voice for a Life of Meaning and Joy* (New York: HarperCollins Publisher, 2019), chapter 2, Kindle.
20. Amy Morin, *13 Things Mentally Strong People Don't Do: Take Back Your Power, Embrace Change, Face Your Fears, and Train Your Brain for Happiness and Success* (New York: HarperCollins Publisher, 2014), chapter 7.
21. Morin, *Mentally Strong People*, chapter 9.

aside ten minutes a week to sincerely congratulate other people on things that are going well for them. You'll be surprised at how much joy will inevitably flow into your life. Learn to be happy for other people's wins, and you'll multiply your happiness potential by infinity.

10. **Don't hate yourself.** Self-hate is often the most common symptom of low mental health, so let's dig into this one a little more. In the English language, *love* and *hate* are both nouns and verbs, which may be why we generally assume *to love* or *to hate* mean to feel something rather than to do something. When it comes to relationships, whether it is with other people or with yourself, the action more often than not precedes the emotion.

A startling example of this phenomenon occurred in an elementary classroom in 1968 in what was meant to be a harmless simulation of racism. In an effort to help her students understand the recent death of Martin Luther King Jr., Jane Elliot had her third-grade students separate themselves into groups based on eye color. For an entire day, anyone with blue eyes was treated as second class. Non-blue-eyed students were able to go first in the drinking fountain line, get extra recess, and exclude blue-eyed students from their lunch table and play. Within a few hours, the non-blue-eyed students felt real contempt and hatred for their blue-eyed classmates. "I watched what had been marvelous, cooperative, wonderful, thoughtful children turn into nasty, vicious, discriminating little third-graders in a space of fifteen minutes," remarked the teacher.[22] Other studies and real-life experiences have repeatedly demonstrated the same point: if you act hateful, you will feel hate.[23]

---

22. "Introduction," Frontline: A Class Divided, PBS, January 1, 2003, https://www.pbs.org/wgbh/frontline/article/introduction-2/.
23. One such study was the Stanford Prison Experiment. Volunteers were randomly selected to be prisoners or guards. The experiment was supposed to run for two weeks but was ended after only six days because of the escalating sadistic behavior of the guards (see "8. Conclusion," The Stanford Prison Experiment, accessed July 14, 2021, https://www.prisonexp.org/conclusion).

The same goes for love. Regardless of how you may *feel* about yourself when in a mental slump, *treat* yourself with love: give yourself the benefit of the doubt, listen to how you feel, allow yourself to do things you enjoy, tell yourself *please* and *thank you*, avoid name calling, and touch your body with kindness *always*. If it helps, create an imaginative cheerleader in your head whose job it is to tell you things you admire about yourself or your accomplishments. Remember, it is hard to love yourself when you treat yourself like dirt, so *be nice*.

No matter what you are feeling, you are not alone. One out of five Americans suffer with mental illness every year.[24] And more importantly, Christ Himself knows what you're going through. He's been where you are and much, much lower. You have a reason to be on this earth. Keep going. Your mental health challenges are more than obnoxious detours keeping you from living your real life. This challenge is just as much a valid life experience as anything else out there. If mental illness keeps you humble and reliant on God, then it may be that mental illness is exactly the thing you need to reach your highest heights. Remember, God gave Moses a speech impediment not to break him, but to make him.[25] Your struggles with mental health can do the same for you.

---

24. National Alliance on Mental Illness, "Mental Health."
25. I think we often overlook the impact having a speech impediment likely had on Moses prior to becoming the leader of Israel. He was probably bullied as a child. He probably experienced a lot of shame or embarrassment. He probably felt less capable than his peers. Yet, it was these characteristics that made him teachable and trainable and receptive to the tutelage of God. Had he not had a physical handicap, it's likely he would have become a full-fledged princely jerk who was uninterested in taking directives from the the Lord. Yes, he may have lived longer in luxury, but he never would have become his sea-parting, life-saving, miracle-making self.

Cut the Shark Music

Worry does not empty tomorrow of its sorrow,
it empties today of its strength.[1]

—CORRIE TEN BOOM;
SURVIVOR, JOY SPREADER, FAITH BUILDER

Even if we know that we, with our superhuman sidekick, will be able to get through whatever life throws at us—brokenness and all—not knowing what's coming or when is enough to drive us all bonkers. It's like living with the *Jaws* theme song playing on repeat in the background. You know the shark is in the water. You know it will attack. But when? Where? Whom? You sweat, breathe, and wait, dying in suspense.

This looming, dark feeling apparently haunts a lot of people, even when fully immersed in their happiest moments. Brené Brown, the famous shame researcher, admits that living joyfully in the moment is a form of vulnerability that most of us will try to avoid. We don't like being vulnerable—subject to risk—and exposed to possible heartache. So to protect ourselves, we allow a constant veil of grief and despair to hang over our otherwise light-, joy-filled lives.[2] Lame, isn't it? Fear and anxiety for the Might Happen won't let us live the Really Happening. It's like whenever I traverse my house in the middle of the night, I'm

---

1. Corrie Ten Boom, *Clippings from My Notebook: Writings and Sayings Collected* (Minneapolis: World Wide Publications, 1984), Internet Archive, 33, https://archive.org/details/clippingsfrommyn00tenb.
2. Brené Brown, *Daring Greatly: How the Courage to Be Vulnerable Transforms the Way We Live, Love, Parent, and Lead* (New York, NY: Gotham Books, 2012), 117–126.

so positive that *tonight* is the night someone decides to break into my home and pounce on me when I am least expecting it. I won't let it happen, though. I won't be caught off guard. So I psych myself up that there really is someone in my house and, with heavy object in hand, brace myself for their pop-and-scare entrance around every corner. It's a ridiculous way to live.

When God told the Saints, "Be still and know that I am God,"[3] they were right in the middle of the infamous Missouri persecution. A few months earlier, their printing house had been destroyed, their Church leaders tarred and feathered, and many others driven from their homes. In the next few years, they would go on to experience even worse persecution, including Governor Boggs's Extermination Order and the death and carnage of the Haun's Mill Massacre. God knew terrible things were heading their way, but "freak out and worry constantly about it" was not how He advised the Saints to handle it.[4]

Many of Brené's clients admitted that putting off feelings of joy so as not to be caught off guard by the future was one of their biggest regrets. When many of them looked back, they wished they had enjoyed the good while they had it instead of constantly worrying about the possible unknowns.[5] This is relevant advice for all of us, as anxiety is quickly becoming the dominant emotion of current earth-dwellers, leading many psychologists to refer to our time as The Age of Anxiety.[6]

Reminding yourself that tomorrow may just as easily bring unforeseeable joy as misery can help hush your fears of the future. You never know, the best thing that has ever happened to you could be right around the corner. From an early age, Elizabeth Barrett had consigned herself to a lonely, secluded life cloistered in the dark upstairs

---

3. D&C 101:16.
4. This is also true of how Christ advised His disciples to act when, unbeknown to them, His death and burial were right around the corner. "Let not your heart be troubled, neither let it be afraid" (John 14:27).
5. Brown, *Daring Greatly*, 117–126.
6. Jean M. Twenge, "The Age of Anxiety? The Birth Cohort Change in Anxiety and Neuroticism, 1952–1993" *Journal of Personality and Social Psychology* 79, no. 6 (2000): 1007.

bedroom of her parents' home.[7] Despite the efforts that the best medicine Victorian England could offer, a reoccurring sickness had left her with a weak heart, lungs, and permanently damaged spine.[8] Although she kept her mind active through reading and writing, by her late thirties, Elizabeth felt death was all that was left for her in life. Oh, how wrong she was. After publishing a poem[9] praising three popular poets of the day, one of them, Robert Browning, responded: "I love your verses with all my heart, dear Miss Barrett . . . and I love you.[10] Please, can I meet you?"[11]

"No," she said. "I'm ugly and sickly and you'll be disappointed."

So they wrote letters to each other—for a year.[12, 13] Robert continued to beg to meet her, but how could she let him? Without a doubt, Elizabeth looked better on paper. But, finally she agreed. Carried down the stairs to the visiting room, Elizabeth waited anxiously for Robert to arrive. *He'll take one look at me and leave. I don't want to be in love anyway. What a waste of time. I should have stayed upstairs. What was I thinking??*

Elizabeth's shark music was playing at full force. But unnecessarily. Robert arrived with fresh-picked flowers in hand[14] and after meeting her was more in love than ever.[15] In true Victorian fashion

---

7. Kathleen E. Royds, *Browning and Her Poetry* (London: George G. Harrap & Co. 1923), 37.
8. Wilcox, *10 Great Souls,* 216, 220.
9. Wilcox, *10 Great Souls,* 218. The poem was entitled "Lady Geraldine's Courtship." It was published in 1844 within a collection entitled *Poems.* ("Elizabeth Barret Browninøg," Poets.org, accessed June 30, 2021, https://poets.org/poet/elizabeth-barrett-browning).
10. Elizabeth Barret Browning," *Britannica,* accessed June 25, 2021, https://www.britannica.com/biography/Elizabeth-Barrett-Browning. "[10 January 1845]. Browning, Robert to Browning, Elizabeth Barrett," Baylor University Library Digital Collections, accessed May 14, 2021, https://digitalcollections-baylor.quartexcollections.com/Documents/Detail/10-january-1845.-browning-robert-to-browning-elizabeth-barrett./342166?item=342169.
11. He didn't ask to meet her in his first letter. In his second letter he alludes to meeting her in the Spring.
12. Wilcox, *10 Great Souls,* 219.
13. Wilcox, 222.
14. Wilcox, 220.
15. Wilcox, 94.

Robert waited until he was home and then penned a letter popping the question, "Will you marry me?"[16]

Elizabeth did the scariest thing she had ever done—let her joy of the present trump her fears of the future—and said yes. They were married within two weeks and moved to the warm coasts of Italy in hopes that the fresh air would strengthen Elizabeth's lungs.[17] When Elizabeth passed away fifteen years later[18] with Robert and their son, Pen, by her bedside, she marveled at how her life had unexpectedly become so full of joy. Her last word captured it all: "Beautiful."[19, 20]

Don't let your worries about tomorrow ruin your chance to enjoy today. Yes, trials suck. They are never enjoyable. They try your soul in every uncomfortable way. But they all lead, eventually, to one outcome—joy. As we believe this more completely, we can live with confident tranquility because we know that even tumultuous times will be overcome, and there is nothing—*nothing*—that can mess up God's plan. As Corinthians 2:9 reminds us, "Eye hath not seen, nor ear heard, neither has entered into the heart of men the things that God has prepared for them that love him."

Learn to live in the open, susceptible to whatever comes your way, and be okay with it. These tips may help:

- Ask yourself, "If I weren't anxious about this situation, how would I feel about it?" You might be surprised that the feelings beneath your angst may be quite different than the fear and nervousness that tend to take center stage. Give yourself a chance to let your other emotions shine brighter than your anxiety.
- Set up "worrying time" in your day when you are allowed to worry about anything and everything. It doesn't matter how irrational or unlikely your fears are. Spend time sitting and wallowing with them. When your time is up, leave your worries

---

16. Wilcox, 220. He sent the letter a couple of days after their meeting.
17. Wilcox, 99.
18. Wilcox, 229.
19. Wilcox, 231.
20. I present a paraphrased version of their story. The real thing is much more romantic. I encourage you to read it.

there and walk away. Don't allow yourself to worry about future events until your next scheduled worry time.
- When your mind starts to run away from you, tune in to your body. How do your toes feel? What are the tense places on your body? How does the breeze feel against your cheek? Taking a quick check on your bodily status does wonders for slowing your mind down and making you stay in the present.
- Do things that you are afraid of or worry about. This teaches us that reality is not as scary or risky as we often believe it to be. The more we do things we are afraid of, the more our confidence in ourselves (and in our sidekick's power to help us) grows, which helps us call out the lies that our fears try to sell us on.
- Do the Shadrack, Meshack, and Abendiago—hope for the best, but know that the worst will be okay, too. (We know that God will save us, *but if not*, it's okay. I'm confident we will be safe, *but if not*, we'll get through it)[21]

As Christ's disciples we are promised an abundant life, but often we stop ourselves from experiencing that blessing by filling our hearts and minds with unneeded worry and anxiety. Look to Christ and live. Look to Christ and believe that although horrible, bad things could happen any and every moment of the day, you know that whatever does happen will "be for your good,"[22] that God "will be on your right hand and on your left,"[23] and that He will help you overcome it. Look to Christ and live joyfully.

---

21. Daniel 3:17–18.
22. D&C 122:7.
23. D&C 84:88.

Snip, Snip, Ouch!

But these facts and opinions look so similar![1]

—JOY; INSIDE OUT CHARACTER

"Blasphemy!"
"Burn him!"
"God hater!"
These were some of the acidic charges Galileo heard during his trial with the Catholic Inquisition in 1633. They didn't burn him, but they did put him under house arrest for the rest of his life.[2]

Why the mean vibes?

Galileo was one of the first scientists to insist that the sun, not the earth, lay at the middle of the solar system. This created a faith crisis.

How so?

When Old Testament hero Joshua[3] was fighting the Amorites, he asked God to make the sun stand still, which He did. How could God make the sun stand still if it wasn't moving in the first place? Not only that, but several Bible passages plainly state that the earth stands still and does not move.[4] As people in the 1600s saw it, either Galileo was right or the scriptures were.

Today, it's easy for us to accept a sun-centered universe *and* scriptures that are true. We didn't grow up thinking otherwise and never had to shift our paradigms to include that new information. But just

---

1. *Inside Out*, directed by Pete Docter (Walt Disney Studios Motion Pictures, 2015), 1:42:00.
2. Peter Machamer and David Marshall Miller, "Galileo Galilei," *The Stanford Encyclopedia of Philosophy*, 2021, https://plato.stanford.edu/entries/galileo/.
3. Joshua 10:13.
4. 1 Chronicles 16:30, Psalm 93:1, Psalm 96:10, Psalm 104:5, Ecclesiastes 1:5.

like the Galileo haters, we are constantly facing new information that can either threaten or build our faith in God.

Imagine that you have a belief garden full of trees that represent different beliefs you hold. Some of these beliefs will grow strong and sturdy and mature into knowledge trees. Others will start to grow but then wither and die. Just like the gardener of the vineyard analogy in Jacob 5, it's your job to upkeep and prune your belief garden. You will have to find the beliefs that are filling your garden with rotten, foul-smelling fruit and uproot them and throw them away. Sometimes pulling out one of these trees can be painful and shake up the root systems of nearby trees in your garden. Often this results in a faith crisis as you learn that things aren't the way you thought they were.

Just like the people in the 1600s who built an understanding of God around their astronomical belief that the earth was in the center of the universe, we also create paradigms of the world based on our current but incomplete knowledge of how it all works. It's human nature. But we need to be okay with getting it wrong sometimes and having to expand our paradigms when we gather new information. Today our testimonies are not threatened by the fact that the sun is in the middle of the universe, but many testimonies are threatened by scientific research on evolution, unsettling actions of past prophets, or changing Church practices. Sometimes I hear people say, "I can't be a member of the Church anymore because now I know X." Well, why not? Why are you putting God in a box and telling Him there's only one way reality can be? Don't let your knowledge tree die just because your beliefs are corrected. Allow your understanding of His world to grow and change as you gain more knowledge and experience.

Modifying your beliefs and shifting your paradigm as you gain more experience and knowledge can be hard, even painful. Most of the time belief pruning requires spiritual and emotional labor, and it always, *always* requires humble communication with God.[5] As I was writing

---

5. Stephan C. Harper gave a great BYU devotional on the type of labor that is involved in seeking truth. He also gives examples of how you have to prune beliefs by adjusting your definitions of certain things. For example, we may initially believe that a revelator is a near-perfect person who receives information from God but with experience modify our definition to a person who receives information from God. (See Stephen C. Harper, "How I Became a Seeker," BYU devotional address, June 8, 2021, https://speeches.byu.edu/talks/steven-c-harper/how-i-became-a-seeker/.)

this chapter, I did a quick survey of family, friends, and acquaintances about beliefs they had to prune out of their gardens that proved to be untrue as they got older. Here's a sampling of what they said:

- Latter-day Saints own the truth and no one else has any idea what they are doing.
- Being gay is a sin.
- Dating ends with finding your soul mate, and marriage begins with living happily ever after.
- There's only one way to be a righteous Latter-day Saint woman.
- Non-members are unhappy and miserable.
- Evolution and a Supreme Creator are conflicting ideas.
- A mother who works is a bad mother.
- Black skin is a curse from God.
- Prophets are perfect and live flawless lives.
- Joseph Smith had only one wife.
- If you smoke or drink coffee, you are a bad person.
- Polygamy was a solution to take care of the widowed and poor.
- Only priesthood holders can pray in meetings with both men and women.
- The priesthood = men in the covenant.
- Righteous people are people who never sin.
- Joseph Smith only wrote one version of the First Vision.
- Modesty is a law for women about what they can or cannot wear.
- You should only eat meat in the winter.
- If I am righteous, bad things will never happen to me.

Some of these discarded beliefs may seem simplistic, insignificant, narrow-minded, or bigoted now, but for many of the people I spoke to, removing these beliefs from their belief garden was a spiritually tormenting process. Like pro-earth-centered universe folk, one or more of these beliefs helped them understand many others. For example, when my mother was a child in the 1950s, she asked why Blacks could not hold the priesthood. She was told that the priesthood was a very heavy responsibility and that to people incapable of keeping its responsibilities it would be a curse. When my mother grew up and met and befriended many capable, smart, responsible Black people, she realized that her childhood belief couldn't be true. But if that wasn't true, why *couldn't* Blacks have the priesthood? Removing that belief left a rift in my mother's belief garden that sent her back on the spiritual journey of asking questions and seeking answers.

On your learning and growing journey, be careful not to reject one belief in order to accept a new one too quickly. Three years before I was born, the anti-Mormon world exploded with glee. The Salamander Letter surfaced, which proved, or at least cast considerable evidence on, the kookiness of the Church origin story.[6] *Haha, suckers. Here's even more proof you're all crazy!* For many Saints, the letter undermined their idea of how Joseph Smith found the plates, and so they left the Church. A year later the letter was proven a fake.[7] *Oops.* But then you had people question President Benson's role as prophet. *Shouldn't he have been able to know the letter was a fake?* And so others left. Instead of refining their understandings of a prophet—old or new—they dumped the idea altogether.

If you don't have all the information and yet you have to keep pruning and refining your belief garden, how can you be sure of anything? How do you know if something is a belief or knowledge? Or if you've got it wrong or right? Here are three rules of thumb to go about knowing what beliefs to keep and which to cast away:

1. **Look for the principle**. Metaphors change and paradigms shift, but principles are eternal. Look for what you can keep before throwing away what doesn't work anymore. Through

---

6. The Salamander Letter was forged by Mark Hofmann, made re-infamous by the Netflix documentary *Murder among the Mormons*. Presumedly written by Martin Harris, the letter describes Joseph being led to the plates on Hill Cumorah by a magical white salamander instead of an angel.
7. Gordon B. Hinckley, "Keep the Faith," *Ensign*, September 1985, https://www.churchofjesuschrist.org/study/ensign/1985/09/keep-the-faith?lang=eng.
Dallin H. Oaks, "Recent Events Involving Church History and Forged Documents," *Ensign*, October 1987, https://www.churchofjesuschrist.org/study/ensign/1987/10/recent-events-involving-church-history-and-forged-documents?lang=eng.

experience and time, you will find that God is the same yesterday, today, and tomorrow, and while your knowledge garden has exploded with growth, the core stuff hasn't really changed.

2. **Test the fruits.** Faith is not knowledge. We aren't *supposed* to know it all, but God does ask us to try our best. We can make our best guess by looking at the fruits of whatever belief we are investigating. The fruits you are looking for are feelings of love, joy, peace, kindness, patience, goodness, faith, gentleness, and self-control.[8] How does that belief make you feel? How does it motivate you to act? Does it reflect the spirit of the beatitudes?

3. **Ask God.**[9] Let Him know what information you are looking for and what questions you have. The stronger your personal relationship with Him, the easier it will be for you to discern which parts of your belief garden you need to hang on to and which parts you need to let go of or modify. If your attachment to God is tenuous, you'll either become defensive when things appear to challenge your beliefs or avoid information that could prove you wrong. Neither is healthy.[10] A secure, strong attachment to God allows you to be intellectually and

---

8. Galatians 5:22–23.
9. A great example of this in practice is the Christofferson family and how they treated their gay son, Tom. In a time when many Latter-day Saint families were shaming or denouncing their gay children, the Christoffersons felt compelled to do the opposite. Through prayer and communion with God, they realized that "the only thing [they could] really be perfect at is loving each other." And so they kept Tom within their circle of love and acceptance despite the cultural norm of the time (see Tom Christofferson, *That We May Be One: A Gay Mormon's Perspective on Faith and Family* [Salt Lake City, Utah: Deseret Book, 2017], 24, Kindle).
10. Psychologists have found that those who have a strong attachment and are secure in relationships more easily confront and deal with information that changes or challenges their belief system. Those who have weak attachments tend to have cognitive rigidity which makes it hard to accept or address information that conflicts with their current opinions. They will either become aggressive or avoidant (see Begley, *Train Your Mind*, 195).

spiritually inquisitive in a way that leaves you open to learning and growth. Trust Him. Turn to Him. He will guide you.

Compared to the knowledge and wisdom of God, we know so little. Knowing too little but thinking they knew it all was the biggest hang-up the Pharisees ran into when the Son of God Himself came down to bring them up to heaven. He didn't look like they expected. He didn't talk like they thought He should. He didn't fit into the box their previous study and experience had created for Him. So they rejected Him and lost out on so much.

You're not going to get it right all the time. Focus more on going the right direction than getting the right details. Do the best you can with the knowledge you have, and when you get something wrong, *which you will*, don't throw out the baby with the bath water. You risk missing out on the greater reality that God is anxious to share with you.

I Was Born to Do This

Frodo: "I wish the ring had never come to me."
Gandolf: "So do all who live to see such times, but that is not for them to decide. All we have to decide is what to do with the time that is given to us."[1]

After seven hours and 2,803 miles of travel, my car pulled up to La Casa del Amor Birth Center in the untamed jungle of the Yucatan Peninsula. Rafaela, barely topping five-foot-two and dressed in a traditional Mayan floral shirt, came out to greet us. Sitting in the covered bamboo pavilion to the side of her house while her granddaughter served tortilla chips sprinkled with fresh lime juice, I heard her story.

Rafaela had lived in the same village her whole life. Like most people in her village, she grew up speaking Mayan and never expected to learn a different language, let alone to read or write. Until recently, her small village had no paved roads, no electricity, no indoor plumbing. Horseback was the quickest way of transportation. Rafaela was married at fifteen and by nineteen had four children. She was happy and content and didn't expect much more out of her simple yet familiar life. But then she started having dreams of delivering babies. At first these dreams seemed so ridiculous that they were funny, but then they started to scare her. Why was she having these dreams? What was God trying to tell her? Did He really want her to become a midwife?

---

1. *The Lord of the Rings: The Fellowship of the Ring*, directed by Peter Jackson (New Line Cinema, 2001), 2:58:00.

Impossible! I know nothing about midwifery! I only speak Mayan. I've never been to school. No, God, I can't do that. Are you crazy? Find somebody else.

Still the impressions persisted. While visiting a friend one day, an old woman came to the door asking for alms. Before she left, she turned to Rafaela and asked her what was bothering her. Rafaela told her about the dreams.

"You already know what you have to do," answered the old woman, and she left.

Soon after, Rafaela had another dream. She saw her Heavenly Father sitting on a throne in front of her. She knelt before Him and, placing her head on His lap, asked Him, "Is it true? Do you really want me to be a midwife? Then, help me."

He laid his hands on her head and gave her the blessing she desired. A few days later, a neighbor came asking for help for his laboring wife. Rafaela went to help. Surprisingly, thanks to the dreams, she knew exactly what she needed to do. Later the city asked for volunteers to be trained as midwives in their local communities in order to improve natal care to women there. Rafaela was selected from her community, but she was sent home after only a few weeks; she already knew everything they taught in the course. Since that time, Rafaela has worked as a midwife, helping not only the Mayan women in her village but also women all around the Yucatan Peninsula and beyond. Her reputation has crossed borders and nations, and women from all over the world frequently attend the workshops that she hosts from her ancestral home in Izamel, Mexico.[2]

God may ask us to do things we don't want to do, are terrified of doing, or didn't plan on doing. Letting God take over the driver seat of your life is never easy. Elder Holland talked about this process: "In those crucial moments of pivotal personal history [we must] submit ourselves to God even when all our hopes and fears may tempt us otherwise. We must be willing to place all that we have—not just our possessions . . . but also our ambitions and pride and stubbornness

---

2. Rafaela Can Ake, personal communication, January 2021.

and vanity—on the altar of God, kneel there in silent submission, and willingly walk away."[3]

Although submitting to God's call may feel like an unjustified sacrifice, many people have found that doing so leads them to discover a deeper, more fulfilling purpose of being. We don't know a lot about what happened before we got to this floating rock of ours, but we do know that the transition from spirit person to human person required one thing of us: a covenant. A covenant to come here and do something to help push along Mother and Father's plan of helping Their kids improve and get back home.[4] Thanks to a divine dose of amnesia, we don't remember what that covenant is once we get here. Yet, spiritual promptings, inner voices, even innate desires help us find the way. As President Spencer W. Kimball taught: "Before we came [to earth, we] were given certain assignments. . . . While we do not now remember the particulars, this does not alter the glorious reality of what we once agreed to."[5]

People have called the symptoms of this premortal covenant a variety of things—a calling, a duty, a mission, a vocation. Its nudging presence has been talked about and expressed throughout the writings of human history (not to mention being a core theme of almost every Disney movie ever made, from *The Lion King* to *Coco*). An Indian spiritual text from around 300 B.C., the *Bhagavad Gita*, calls this

---

3. Jeffery R. Holland and Patricia T. Holland, *On Earth As It Is in Heaven* (Salt Lake City: Desert Book, 1989), 128.
4. Carol F. McConkie, "Here to Serve a Righteous Cause," October 2015 general conference, https://www.churchofjesuschrist.org/study/general-conference/2015/10/here-to-serve-a-righteous-cause?lang=eng. "Before we were born, we accepted our Heavenly Father's plan "by which [we] could obtain a physical body and gain earthly experience to progress toward perfection and ultimately realize [our] divine destiny as heirs of eternal life." Of this premortal covenant, Elder John A. Widtsoe explained: "We agreed, right then and there, to be not only saviors for ourselves but . . . saviors for the whole human family. We went into a partnership with the Lord. The working out of the plan became then not merely the Father's work, and the Savior's work, but also our work. The least of us, the humblest, is in partnership with the Almighty in achieving the purpose of the eternal plan of salvation.'"
5. Spencer W. Kimball, "The Role of Righteous Women," October 1979 general conference, https://www.churchofjesuschrist.org/study/general-conference/1979/10/the-role-of-righteous-women?lang=eng.

preordained duty your *dharma*. The central story of the Gita follows the ethical dilemmas of Arjuna, a righteous prince, and his mentor, Krishna, God in human form. With patience and love, Krishna helps Arjuna understand key components of dharma. He teaches that pursuing our divine duty with all our gusto is the only way to find success and fulfillment in our earth life. Ignoring or avoiding its demands will leave us deficient and in opposition with ourselves. When Arjuna wishes that he had a different role to play than that of a prince, Krishna cautions him that coveting someone else's path is not only pointless but sinful. In fact, it is better to try and fail at the task God has given us than to fulfill perfectly the task given to someone else.[6, 7]

In his personal and professional experience, Dr. Viktor Frankl found that those who find purpose in their unsolicited circumstances are able to handle what life throws at them better than those who don't. At twenty-four years old, Frankl found himself imprisoned in the Auschwitz Nazi concentration camp. His wife was dead. His research was destroyed. His future was bleak. It was not the life he had wanted for himself. Yet, it was his life. And he realized in the midst of the suffering, misery, and death that his usual go-to question of "What can I ask of life?" was not applicable in this situation. In fact, answering that question at a time when so little of his life was within his control only led to feelings of anger, despair, and victimhood. Instead, the only question he could ask and still come off conqueror was, "What is life asking of me?" By asking this question, he and his fellow prisoners were able to rise up and deal with their suffering with a deep sense of meaning and purpose—even if the answer was only to suffer with grace before unavoidable death.[8]

To be honest, I hate asking, "What is life asking of me?" It's much more fun to answer the former, "What can I ask of life?" But

---

6. This summary of the *Bhagavad Gita* was explained to me through the reading of *The Great Work of Your Life* by Stephen Cope. Stephen Cope, *The Great Work of Your Life: A Guide for the Journey to Your True Calling* (New York: Bantam Books, 2012).
7. The *Bhagavad Gita* is a long, complex text with varying degrees of quality translations. I do not feign to be an expert of the text, but these are my takeaways from my brief study on the subject.
8. Viktor E. Frankl, *Man's Search for Meaning* (Boston, MA: Beacon Press, 1984), 96–98.

sometimes asking the first question is the only way to find peace in what happens to you and to discover the path that leads to fulfilling your calling.

God crashing my life plans is the reason I'm writing this book in the first place. Nine months ago, I went all out on executing my Life Goal #3—Travel World with Fam. I visualized. I researched. I planned and took action. Visa application? Check. Housing secured? Check. Job quit? Check. Itinerary of awesome adventures planned? Check. But then, it didn't happen. Like a house of cards, all of my plans, efforts, and visions came tumbling down. My health plummeted. My finances plunged. My dreams nose-dived. Frustrated and bewildered, I fought to get to the place where I could ask God why the heck I was still in Vineyard, Utah, and not gallivanting across Mexico. In other words, "What is life asking of me right now?" He gave me some things to work on. Improve family relationships. Firm up my attachment to Him. Quit being so prideful. Be a better neighbor. Write that book.

I wish I could say it's been an easy path to submit to. It hasn't. Yet, when I let my faith in God's goodness lead, I am filled with light and the disappointment is easier to bare. Regardless, as our friend Enzio Busche once said, when God takes something away, it's only because He has something better to give you.[9] I believe that.

Don't be surprised if your God-prompted mission changes during different stages of your life. Right now God might just be asking you to be the best student you can be. Or you might be in a stage where God encourages you to pursue your innate desires. Or He's just preparing you for the time to go full-throttle at sharing your unique gifts with the world.

For almost twenty years, Angela Johnson dedicated her life to music. She taught classes at BYU, put on dramatic presentations, and worked tirelessly to obtain her goal of becoming an opera singer. For

---

9. F. Enzio Busche, "Unleashing the Dormant Spirit," BYU Speeches, May 14, 1996, https://kevinhinckley.com/userfiles/files/busche_fenzio_1996_05.pdf. "When you are compelled to give up something or when things that are dear to you are withdrawn from you, know that this is your lesson to be learned right now. But know also that, as you are learning this lesson, God wants to give you something better" (7).

much of her life, God supported this path, and she blessed many people along the way. However, one day God asked her to change. During her typical four-hour voice training, Angela had a piercing impression that she would never attain her goal of singing in the Metropolitan Opera. After receiving that witness, she felt that something had broken inside her. She drove to the craft store and—for whatever reason—picked up a lump of clay and a stylus. Returning home, she molded her internal suffering—a bust of a young girl crying in pain. Although Angela had never molded clay before, she felt that testifying of Christ through sculpting was what God was calling her to dedicate the rest of her life to. *She answered.* During the next two decades, Angela created dozens of exhibits, including the world's largest sculptural collection of Christ's life. She has become a world-renown sculptor, and you can see her work on display at a permanent destination in the Thanksgiving Point Ashton Botanical Gardensin Lehi, Utah. [10]

---

10. Bob Mims, "Mormon Sculptor Pours Her Passion and Pain into a Monumental Display," *The Salt Lake Tribune*, June 21, 2017, https://archive.sltrib.com/article.php?id=5345866&itype=CMSID. Jeanette Bennett, "State of the Art: Angela Johnson Sculpts Christ's Life in Thanksgiving Point's Light of the World Garden," Utah Valley 360, August 7, 2016, https://utahvalley360.com/2016/08/07/state-art-angela-johnson-sculpts-christs-life-thanksgiving-points-light-world-garden/. LOTWF, "Angela Johnson Story—Light of the World Garden," YouTube video, 3:12, October, 20, 2016, https://www.youtube.com/watch?v=nnthnRNnBV0&t=1s. Another example of this is Janice Kapp Perry. Perry has written more than 3,000 songs, many of which are in the Church Primary songbook, such as "I Love to See the Temple," "Love Is Spoken Here," "A Child's Prayer," "We'll Bring the World His Truth," and many more. If anyone were to guess what her calling on earth is they'd quickly say music. But Janice didn't start writing music until she was nearly forty. In fact, after she finished her music major at BYU, she did very little with music for twenty years. Instead, she worked in a potato shed, raised four children, competed in community sports, and worked as a typist. You'd think with talent like hers, God would have been pressing her to write music right after leaving the womb, but He didn't. You will have different stages and phases for the work you do here on earth. See Aaron Sorenson, "Prolific Composer and Songwriter Janice Kapp Perry Awarded Honorary Doctorate Degree," *BYU News*, April 23, 2020, https://news.byu.edu/character/prolific-composer-and-songwriter-janice-kapp-perry-awarded-honorary-doctorate-degree. Charlene Renberg, "A Testimony Through Song," Y Magazine, Summer 2013, https://magazine.byu.edu/article/a-testimony-through-song/.

Your ages and stages will demand different things from you. Be patient yet persistent in doing God's will. When things don't go as planned, lean into what life asks of you. When you hear God challenge you to take a new direction, step into the darkness. When a dream is postponed or a fear brought head-on, rise up and bear it with Christ. You were made for more than you can imagine, and leaning into God's call will help you do and become more than you ever thought possible.

Be the Good

Every man gives his life
for what he believes.
Every woman gives her life
for what she believes.
Sometimes people believe
in little or nothing,
and so they give their lives
to little or nothing.[1]

—JOAN OF ARC; DOER, BELIEVER, DISCIPLE

"Is this the guy I am supposed to marry?"
"Is BYU the right school for me?"
"Should I major in humanities or something more job applicable?"
"Am I meant to serve a mission?"
"Will this new job take me to where I need to end up?"

These are all questions that I have asked during my life when I was seeking God's guidance to fulfill my divine mission. But guess what answers I got to all of those questions? Nothing. Nil. Nada. These

---

1. Maxwell Anderson, *Joan of Lorraine: A Play in Two Acts* (Dramatists Play Service, January 1974) act 2, interlude 3, 80. This quote is from a play about Joan of Arc spoken by the character who plays Joan of Arc moments before she is consumed by the flames that take her life. Although this quote is not historical, I believe the quote captures Joan's unbreakable faith that led her to be the heroine she became. The rest of the quote is just as powerful: "One life is all we have, and we live it as we believe in living it, and then it's gone. But to surrender what you are, and live without belief—that's more terrible than dying—more terrible than dying young."

139

were really big and significant questions. God had given me specific feedback on crossroads before. Why not now?

The divine silence in these instances was shattering. I liked to believe that along with giving each of us a mission to complete here on earth, God had also created an elaborate and detailed supposed-to-be-plan and that all I had to do was to come down and follow it step by step to achieve my eternal realm of awesomeness. I was especially enamored by the idea of God leading me to my "soul mate." That one person on all the earth who had been crafted specifically for me. I just knew that finding that one person was essential to me fulfilling my destiny. A significant portion of my adolescence was spent giggling with girlfriends about the man who was out there—somewhere—waiting for me to find him, or, more romantically put, passionately trying to find me.

Welp, I was wrong. When I got to that and other significant choices in my life, God didn't seem to care much about which choice I made. I had to reluctantly uproot the belief that God's call includes predetermined details of each step of our lives or that our job is to merely follow the fated path. Instead, I've learned that, while at times God may ask us to do specific things, our divine callings allow for a wide range of actions, choices, and life plans—all while remaining within the umbrella of fulfilling our pre-earth-life covenant. Rather than a pre-written script we are supposed to continually guess at, we are more like coproducers taking turns with God to craft the details and together create something truly beautiful and unique.

Regardless if God is nudging you down a certain path or letting you take the lead, you can carry out your premortal covenant each step of the way by consecrating your path to be and do good. President Gordon B. Hinckley taught this purpose-driven lifestyle in a devotional to BYU students in 1996. "You are good. But it is not enough just to be good. You must be good for something. You must contribute good to the world. The world must be a better place for your presence. And the good that is in you must be spread to others."[2]

---

2. Gordon B. Hinckley, "Stand Up for Truth," BYU devotional address, September 17, 1996, https://speeches.byu.edu/talks/gordon-b-hinckley/stand-truth/.

Whether or not God is currently calling you to lead armies, save Middle Earth from impending doom, change your career, carry a particularly daunting burden, or postpone life plans, you can always use your time and skills to create a maximum amount of good whatever your circumstance.[3] Although at times God may ask you to take a certain path, most of the time it is possible for you to fulfill your life mission in a variety of situations. To do this, assess your current context and abilities and ask, "How can I make a positive impact in the world around me right now?" As you do so, you will find that you can "lift up the hands which hang down, and strengthen the feeble knees"[4] as a nurse, a teacher, an accountant, an Uber driver, a sister, a traveler, a neighbor, an anything.

One way to add good in the world anytime, anywhere is to raise your voice for light, truth, and Christ. During a testimony meeting where he was presiding, Elder Bednar gave a very simple yet profound lesson on the giving of testimonies. He taught that testimonies are simple and should focus on the five cornerstones of our faith—belief in Heavenly Father, Jesus Christ, Joseph Smith, the Book of Mormon, and the current leaders of our Church. He then challenged us to bear our testimonies focused on only those five things. To be honest, I was skeptical and promptly hunkered down for a repetitive and boring testimony meeting. Shock and surprise: it was awesome! Every word was said with conviction and feeling. There was no fluff, random asides, or endless thank-i-monies. Each testimony reaffirmed and strengthened the ones that came before. It was impossible to leave that meeting without having your own testimony strengthened in at least one of those five cornerstones.

That experience made me realize that one voice raised in union with another kindles incredible power. God doesn't need our words to be unique; He needs our words to be true. And to inundate the world with our stories. The latest social reform movements were so successful

---

3. Elder S. Gifford Nielson gave a great definition of a calling: "Do the greatest possible good with the talents and gifts we have." S. Gifford Nielsen, "This Is Our Time!" April 2021 general conference, https://www.churchofjesuschrist.org/study/general-conference/2021/04/33nielsen?lang=eng.
4. D&C 81:5.

not because of the uniqueness of the participants' stories but because of the abundance of their similarities. Each voice—*your voice*—adds weight to the scale pushing truth upward to clear the clouds of misconceptions and help us all better understand reality. When talking with friends, when posting on social media, when meeting strangers at the beach, use your voice to speak truth and light.

You are a powerful creator. You have the ability to make things happen. To do big and crazy, impossible things. You can choose to follow whatever desires show up in your heart and to create the life of your dreams. It is up to you. But in all of that desiring and choosing and creating, will you choose to do it with Christ? You don't have to. You have the capacity to make your life all about you and to find all kinds of success while doing that. You can make millions of dollars, buy acres of real estate, and spend hours of your days reposing on the beach. You don't have to spend one minute thinking about heaven, eternity, or the progression of your soul. But God offers you a more excellent way.

Christ once called His people the salt of the earth. If that's true, then as you partner with Him, your life will become more flavorful, more colorful, and more meaningful than you've ever imagined. His way requires listening, humility, patience, relationships, partnership, even submission. But the reward is out of this world—complete transformation, complete power, complete knowledge, complete wisdom, complete wholeness. No other reward can even compare with what God has promised you can become. Go for it. Don't stop. Fall down. Get back up. Smile. Cry. Embrace the journey. You only get to do this once. Make the most of it. Be and become you, with God, on purpose.

Appendix

Types of Prayer and What They're Good For

Many different types of prayer exist, and they all play a role in your life. Read through these types and see which ones you need to incorporate into your life more.

The Habit of Looking Up Prayer

This is the prayer you carry with you in your heart. An ongoing conversation you're having with God in your head. Like the Verizon guy from the 90s commercial, you walk a few steps, stop, and ask into the phone, "Can you hear me now?" and then move forward. This type of prayer plays the largest role in developing emotional intimacy and keeping God close to your thoughts.

The O, God, Help Me! Prayer

This prayer happens involuntarily when your back is against the wall and you have nowhere else to turn. It often signifies a turning point where you have become humble enough to ask for help where you weren't before. This prayer is brief but is said with the heart.

The Group Prayer

Praying as a groups unifies those involved around a common feeling or desire. It creates crazy power when everyone involved focuses their faith on one end or objective. The cumulative power is similar to the strength of focusing two square meters of sunlight into a single focal point which can melt any material on earth (Google this. It's mind-blowing).[1] Group prayer leads to miracles.

The Putting It Out There Prayer

Once you've groomed and defined your desires, it's time to put them out there. Let God know. Let His heavenly messengers know. Let the world know. When you express your desires through prayer, not only are you utilizing God's heaven-will-answer guarantee ("Ask and ye shall receive; seek and ye shall find; knock and it shall be opened unto you"[2]), you also align your own internal energy with bringing that desire into fruition.[3] Careful what you ask for, though, because this really works!

The Daily Rhythm Prayer

At set times throughout the day make time to pray no matter what is going on. Typically these prayers are coupled with a habit trigger—sitting down to eat, climbing into bed, getting into the car, and so on. These habitual prayers help you slow down and check in with God when you would normally be on go-go-go mode. Careful, though—they can easily become meaningless if not said with real intent or presence of mind (vain repetitions anyone?).

The Hush, Be Still Prayer

This prayer closely resembles a modern form of mediation. The purpose is to quiet the mind and the body to merely sit with God's spirit. It's best used for quiet, private spaces where it's easy to tune

---

1. BBC, "Jem Melts Rock Using Sunshine—Bang Goes The Theory—Series 3, Episode 5 Preview—BBC One," YouTube video, 1:43, October 1, 2010, https://www.youtube.com/watch?v=z0_nuvPKIi8.
2. Matthew 7:7.
3. Matthew 6:8: "Father knoweth what things ye have need of, before ye ask." Why ask God for things that He already knows you want? Some desires He will not grant until you ask. Also in prayer, you are forced to focus your body, mind, heart, and strength on a singular desire—this intensity and intentionality plays a huge role in bringing your hopes to pass.

out what's going on around you. Sometimes you won't hear anything. Other times, you will receive exactly what you didn't know you needed. This prayer rejuvenates the spirit and brings a lingering feeling of peace and stillness.[4]

The Godly Wrestle Prayer

This prayer is for when you've really got stuff to work through. It could be questions, grief, or desperation. It's best achieved in a quiet, private place where you can pray vocally. Allow for plenty of time. Don't stop until something happens, but beware—this can take hours to days and will be both mentally and physically exhausting. More than other types of prayers, this godly wrestle is transformative. You will come out differently than when you entered. It is usually after this type of prayer that we find the understanding and peace to genuinely say, "Not my will, but thy will be done."

A prayerful life is absolutely required for maintaining close relationships with your Heavenly Parents. If you are feeling far from heaven, there's a good chance upping your prayer game will help. Don't wait to reap the benefits of prayer. Start praying more today.

---

4. This prayer couples beautifully with sitting in the celestial room or other holy places.

Bibliography

The Abraham Lincoln Association, ed. *Collected Works of Abraham Lincoln. Volume 5*. Ann Arbor, Michigan: University of Michigan Digital Library Production Services, 2001. Accessed April 26, 2022. https://quod.lib.umich.edu/cgi/t/text/text-idx?c=lincoln;cc=lincoln;type=simple;rgn=div1;q1=September%2013,%201862;view=text;subview=detail;sort=occur;idno=lincoln5;node=lincoln5:933.

Alcoholics Anonymous World Services. *'Pass It On': The Story of Bill Wilson and How the A. A. Message Reached the World*. New York: Alcoholics Anonymous World Services, Inc., 1984.

Alcott, Louisa May. *Little Women*. Project Gutenberg, 1996. Last updated April 3, 2020. https://www.gutenberg.org/cache/epub/514/pg514-images.html.

Allen, James P. *Middle Egyptian: An Introduction to the Language and Culture of Hieroglyphs*, 2nd ed. Cambridge: Cambridge University Press, 2010, 119–121.

Amy Morin, LSCW. "About." Accessed July 27, 2021, https://amymorinlcsw.com/about-amy/.

Anderson, Jane. "The Impact of Family Structure on the Health of Children: Effects of Divorce." *The Linacre Quarterly*, 81, 4 (2014): 378–87. doi:10.1179/0024363914Z.00000000087.

Anderson, Maxwell. *Joan of Lorraine: A Play in Two Acts*. Dramatists Play Service, January 1974, act 2, interlude 3.

The Arbinger Institute. *The Anatomy of Peace: Resolving the Heart of Conflict*. San Francisco, CA:Berrett-Koehler Publishers, Inc., 2006.

Aristotle. *Nicomachaen Ethics*. Translated by W.D. Ross. The Internet Classics Archive, 350 B.C.E. Accessed July 17, 2021. http://classics.mit.edu/Aristotle/nicomachaen.html.

Babu M G, Ramesh, Rajagopal Kadavigere, Prakashini Koteshwara, Brijesh Sathian, and Kiranmai S. Rai. "Rajyoga Meditation Experience Induces Enhanced Positive Thoughts and Alters Gray Matter Volume of Brain Regions: A Cross-sectional Study." *Mindfulness* 12 (2021): 1659–1671. https://doi.org/10.1007/s12671-021-01630-8.

Ballard, M. Russell. "Return and Receive." April 2017 general conference. https://www.churchofjesuschrist.org/study/general-conference/2017/04/return-and-receive?lang=eng.

Barlow, Nora, ed. *The Autobiography of Charles Darwin*. New York, NY: W.W. Norton & Company, Inc., 1958.

Bascomb, Neal. *The Perfect Mile*. New York: Houghton Mifflin, 2005.

Baylor University Library Digital Collections. "[10 January 1845]. Browning, Robert to Browning, Elizabeth Barrett." Accessed May 14, 2021. https://digitalcollections-baylor.quartexcollections.com/Documents/Detail/10-january-1845.-browning-robert-to-browning-elizabeth-barrett./342166?item=342169.

BBC. "Jem Melts Rock Using Sunshine - Bang Goes The Theory - Series 3, Episode 5 Preview - BBC One." YouTube video, 1:43, October 1, 2010. https://www.youtube.com/watch?v=z0_nuvPKIi8.

Begley, Sharon. *Train Your Mind, Change Your Brain: How a New Science Reveals Our Extraordinary Potential to Transforms Ourselves*. New York: Ballantine Books, 2008.

Benge, Janet and Geoff Benge. *John Newton: Change of Heart*. Seattle, WA: YWAM Publishing, 2018.

Bennett, Jeanette. "State of the Art: Angela Johnson Sculpts Christ's Life in Thanksgiving Point's Light of the World Garden." Utah Valley 360, August 7, 2016. https://utahvalley360.com/2016/08/07/state-art-angela-johnson-sculpts-christs-life-thanksgiving-points-light-world-garden/.

Benson, Ezra Taft. "Cleansing the Inner Vessel." April 1986 general conference. https://www.churchofjesuschrist.org/study/general-conference/1986/04/cleansing-the-inner-vessel?lang=eng.

Bowden, Mark. "'Idiot,' 'Yahoo,' 'Original Gorilla': How Lincoln Was Dissed in His Day: The difficulty of recognizing excellence in its own time." *The Atlantic*, June 2013. https://www.theatlantic.com/magazine/archive/2013/06/abraham-lincoln-is-an-idiot/309304/.

Bradberry, Travis and Jean Greaves. *Emotional Intelligence 2.0*. California: TalentSmart, 2009. Kindle.

Bradford, William. "Of Plymouth Plantation." In *The Norton Anthology of American Literature*, edited by Julia Reidhead, 104–137. New York: Norton & Company, Inc., 2007.

Brannen, Nathan. "Only 1,497 Humans Have Ever Broken the 4-minute Mile — and I'm One of Them." *CBC*, June 27, 2018. https://www.cbc.ca/playersvoice/entry/only-1497-humans-have-ever-broken-the-4-minute-mile-and-im-one-of-them.

Britannica. "Elizabeth Barret Browning." Last updated June 25, 2021. https://www.britannica.com/biography/Elizabeth-Barrett-Browning.

Brown, Brené. *Daring Greatly: How the Courage to Be Vulnerable Transforms the Way We Live, Love, Parent, and Lead*. New York, NY: Gotham Books, 2012.

Brown, Steven and Jenifer Larson-Hall. *Second Language Acquisition Myths: Applying Second Language Research to Classroom Teaching*. Michigan: University of Michigan, 2012.

Burgo, Joseph. "Podcast #509: Good Shame; Bad Shame." Interview with Brett McKay. *The Art of Manliness*. Podcast audio, May 20, 2019. https://www.artofmanliness.com/articles/shame/.

Busche, F. Enzio. "Unleashing the Dormant Spirit." BYU Speeches, May 14, 1996. https://kevinhinckley.com/userfiles/files/busche_fenzio_1996_05.pdf.

Busche, F. Enzio. *Yearning for the Living God: Reflections from the Life of F. Enzio Busche*. Compiled by Tracie A. Lamb. Salt Lake City: Deseret Book, 2004.

C-SPAN. "Presidential Historians Survey 2021." Accessed October 12, 2021. https://www.c-span.org/presidentsurvey2021/?page=overall.

Christofferson, D. Todd. "Gratitude, Responsibility, and Faith." BYU-Idaho Commencement Address, December 21, 2018. https://video.byui.edu/media/Elder+D.+Todd+Christofferson+-+%E2%80%9CGratitude,++Responsibility,+and+Faith%E2%80%9D/1_qc354wqh/84734132.

Christofferson, Tom. *That We May Be One: A Gay Mormon's Perspective on Faith and Family*. Salt Lake City, Utah: Deseret Book, 2017. Kindle.

The Church of Jesus Christ of Latter-day Saints. *Teachings of the Presidents of the Church: David O. McKay.* Salt Lake City: The Church of Jesus Christ of Latter-day Saints, 2011. https://abn.churchofjesuschrist.org/study/manual/teachings-david-o-mckay/chapter-4?lang=eng.

The Church of Jesus Christ of Latter-day Saints. *Teachings of the Presidents of the Church: Joseph F. Smith.* Salt Lake City: The Church of Jesus Christ of Latter-day Saints, 2011. https://www.churchofjesuschrist.org/study/manual/teachings-joseph-f-smith/chapter-33?lang=eng.

Classical Wisdom. "A Tradition of Thumos." June 23, 2014. https://classicalwisdom.com/culture/traditions/tradition-thumos/.

Clear, James. *Atomic Habits: An Easy & Proven Way to Build Good Habits & Break Bad Ones.* New York: Avery, 2018.

Confucious. *The Great Learning.* The Internet Classics Archive, ca 500 B.C.E. Accessed October 15, 2020. http://classics.mit.edu/Confucius/learning.html.

Cope, Stephen. *The Great Work of Your Life: A Guide for the Journey to Your True Calling.* New York: Bantam Books, 2012.

Corbridge, Lawrence E. "Stand Forever." BYU devotional address, January 22, 2019. https://speeches.byu.edu/talks/lawrence-e-corbridge/stand-for-ever/.

Covey, Stephen R. *The Seven Habits of Highly Effective People: Powerful Lessons in Personal Change.* New York: Fireside, 1989.

Craig, Michelle D. "Eyes to See." October 2020 general conference. https://www.churchofjesuschrist.org/study/general-conference/2020/10/14craig?lang=eng.

Cuddy, Amy. *Presence: Bringing Your Boldest Self to Your Biggest Challenges.* New York: Little, Brown Spark, 2015. E-book.

Darwin, Charles. *On the Origin of Species.* London: John Murray, 1872; Project Gutenberg, 1999. https://www.gutenberg.org/files/2009/2009-h/2009-h.htm.

Darwin, Charles. *The Voyage of the Beagle.* New York: New American Library, 1988; Internet Archive. https://archive.org/details/voyageofbeagleme00char/page/436/mode/2up.

BIBLIOGRAPHY

Davis, Tom. "Italian Job-What 'fine' stands for." YouTube video, 0:39, March 17, 2010. https://www.youtube.com/watch?v=KfcrM7ukzCU.

Dew, Sheri. *Insights from a Prophet's Life: Russell M. Nelson*. Salt Lake City: Deseret Book, 2019.

Docter, Pete, director. *Inside Out*. Walt Disney Studios Motion Pictures, 2015. 1:42:00.

Doidge, Norman. *The Brain that Changes Itself: Stories of Personal Triumph from the Frontiers of Brain Science*. New York: Penguin Group, 2007.

Dubey, Akshay. "Healing doesn't mean the damage never existed. It means the damage no longer controls your life..." Goodreads. Accessed October 19, 2021. https://www.goodreads.com/author/quotes/7046878.Akshay_Dubey.

Easwaran, Eknath. *Gandhi the Man: The Story of His Transformation*. California: Nilgiri Press, 1997.

Frankl, Viktor E. *Man's Search for Meaning*. Boston, MA: Beacon Press, 1984.

Freeman, Philip. *St. Patrick of Ireland*. New York, NY: Simon & Schuster, 2004.

Frontline: A Class Divided. "Introduction." PBS, January 1, 2003. https://www.pbs.org/wgbh/frontline/article/introduction-2/.

Gavrilov, Leonid A. and Natalia S. Gavrilova. "Predictors of Exceptional Longevity: Effects of Early-Life Childhood Conditions, Midlife Environment and Parental Characteristics." *Living to 100 Monograph*, 2014: 1–18. https://www.ncbi.nlm.nih.gov/pmc/articles/PMC4318523/.

Givens, Terryl L. and Fiona Givens. *The God Who Weeps: How Mormonism Makes Sense of Life*. The United States of America: Ensign Peak, 2012.

Goad, Kimberly. "What's Race Got to Do with Diabetes?" AARP, November 2, 2018. https://www.aarp.org/health/healthy-living/info-2018/role-of-race-in-diabetes.html#:~:text=African%20Americans%2C%20 Hispanics%2C%20American%20Indians,American%20Diabetes%20 Association%20(ADA).

Google Books Ngram Viewer._https://books.google.com/ngrams/graph?content=virtue&year_start=1800&year_end=2019&corpus=26&smoothing=3&direct_url=t1%3B%2Cvirtue%3B%2Cc0.

BIBLIOGRAPHY

Gottman, John M. and Nan Silver. *The Seven Principles for Making Marriage Work*. New York: Three Rivers Press, 1999.

Grant, Adam. "There's a Name for the Blah You're Feeling: It's Called Languishing." *The New York Times*, April 19, 2021. https://www.nytimes.com/2021/04/19/well/mind/covid-mental-health-languishing.html.

Gray, Karlin. *Serena: The Littlest Sister*. Massachusetts: Page Street Kids, 2019.

Gurmail-Kaufmann, Kira. "7 Things You Need to Know About German Romanticism." *Sotheby's*, November 29, 2018. https://www.sothebys.com/en/articles/7-things-you-need-to-know-about-german-romanticism.

Harper, Stephen C. "How I Became a Seeker." BYU devotional address, June 8, 2021. https://speeches.byu.edu/talks/steven-c-harper/how-i-became-a-seeker/.

Hayes, Stephen C. and Spencer Smith. *Get Out of Your Mind & Into Your Life: The New Acceptance and Commitment Therapy*. Oakland, CA: New Harbinger Publications, Inc, 2005.

Health Encyclopedia. "Journaling for Mental Health." The University of Rochester Medical Center. Accessed July 27, 2021. https://www.urmc.rochester.edu/encyclopedia/content.aspx?ContentID=4552&ContentTypeID=1.

Hillenbrand, Laura. *Unbroken: A World War II Story of Survival, Resilience, and Redemption*. New York: Random House, 2010.

Hinckley, Gordon B. "Closing Remarks." April 2007 general conference. https://abn.churchofjesuschrist.org/study/general-conference/2007/04/closing-remarks?lang=eng.

Hinckley, Gordon B. "How Can I Become the Woman of Whom I Dream?" General Young Women Meeting, April 2001. https://www.churchofjesuschrist.org/study/ensign/2001/05/how-can-i-become-the-woman-of-whom-i-dream?lang=eng.

Hinckley, Gordon B. "Keep the Faith." *Ensign*, September 1985. https://www.churchofjesuschrist.org/study/ensign/1985/09/keep-the-faith?lang=eng.

Hinckley, Gordon B. "Stand Up for Truth." BYU devotional address, September 17, 1996. https://speeches.byu.edu/talks/gordon-b-hinckley/stand-truth/.

Holland, Jeffery R. and Patricia T. Holland. *On Earth As It Is in Heaven*. Salt Lake City: Desert Book, 1989.

Irvine, William B. *A Guide to the Good Life: The Ancient Art of Stoic Joy*. New York: Oxford University, 2008. Kindle.

Isaacson, Walter. *Einstein: His Life and Universe*. New York: Simon and Schuster, 2008.

Itkowitz, Colby. "The Sudden Back-To-Back Deaths of Her Mother and Husband Taught Her 13 Ways Not to Grieve." *The Washington Post*, October 15, 2015. https://www.washingtonpost.com/news/inspired-life/wp/2015/10/15/the-sudden-back-to-back-deaths-of-her-mother-and-husband-taught-her-how-not-to-grieve/.

Jackson, Peter, director. *The Lord of the Rings: The Fellowship of the Ring*. New Line Cinema, 2001. 2:58:00.

Jacobson, Lindsey. "Remembering Nelson Mandela on the Anniversary of His Inauguration." *ABC News*, May 9, 2017. https://abcnews.go.com/International/remembering-nelson-mandela-anniversary-inauguration/story?id=47205398.

Jeffers, Susan. *Feel the Fear…and Do It Anyway*. New York: Ballantine Books, 1987.

Johnson, Jane Clayson. *Silent Souls Weeping: Depression—Sharing Stories, Finding Hope*. Salt Lake City: Deseret Book, 2018. Kindle.

Kaczmarek, Bożydar LJ. "Current Views on Neuroplasticity: What Is New and What Is Old?" *Acta Neuropsychologica* 18, no. 1 (2020).

Kagge, Erling. "Podcast #560: The Magic of Walking." Interview with Brett McKay. *The Art of Manliness*. Podcast audio, November 13, 2019. https://www.artofmanliness.com/articles/benefits-of-walking/.

Kimball, Spencer W. "The Role of Righteous Women." October 1979 general conference. https://www.churchofjesuschrist.org/study/general-conference/1979/10/the-role-of-righteous-women?lang=eng.

Largent, Kimberly J. "Harriet Beecher Stowe: The Little Woman Who Wrote the Book That Started This Great War." The Ohio State University. Accessed October 13, 2021. https://ehistory.osu.edu/articles/harriet-beecher-stowe-little-woman-who-wrote-book-started-great-war.

Lawrence, Larry R. "What Lack I Yet?" October 2015 general conference. https://www.churchofjesuschrist.org/study/general-conference/2015/10/what-lack-i-yet?lang=eng.

Lewis, C. S. *The Abolition of Man in The Complete C. S. Lewis Signature Classics*. New York: HarperCollins, 2002.

Lewis, C. S. *The Last Battle*. New York: Macmillan, 1956; Project Gutenberg Canada, 2014. https://gutenberg.ca/ebooks/lewiscs-lastbattle/lewiscs-lastbattle-00-h.html.

C. S. Lewis, *The Weight of Glory, and Other Addresses*. London: Geoffrey Bles, 1949; Project Gutenberg Canada, 2014. https://gutenberg.ca/ebooks/lewiscs-transposition/lewiscs-transposition-00-h.html.

LOTWF. "Angela Johnson Story - Light of the World Garden." YouTube video, 3:12, October 20, 2016. https://www.youtube.com/watch?v=nnthnRNnBV0&t=1s.

Loy, James D. and Kent M. Loy, *Emma Darwin: a Victorian Life*. Gainesville, FL: University Press of Florida, 2010.

Machamer, Peter and David Marshall Miller. "Galileo Galilei." *The Stanford Encyclopedia of Philosophy*, 2021. https://plato.stanford.edu/archives/sum2021/entries/galileo/.

Mack, Gordon. "2020 Olympic Qualifying Standards Released." *Flotrack*, March 10, 2019. https://www.flotrack.org/articles/6394026-2020-olympic-qualifying-standards-released.

Martin, Denise. "Maat and Order in African Cosmology: A Conceptual Tool for Understanding Indigenous Knowledge." *Journal of Black Studies* 38, no. 6 (2008): 951–67. http://www.jstor.org/stable/40035033.

Martschenko, Daphne. "IQ Tests Have a Dark, Controversial History—but They're Finally Being Used for Good." *Insider*, October 11, 2017. https://www.businessinsider.com/iq-tests-dark-history-finally-being-used-for-good-2017-10#:~:text=The%20first%20of%20these%20tests,basis%20for%20modern%20IQ%20testing.

Maxwell, Neal A. "Swallowed Up in the Will of the Father." October 1995 general conference. https://www.churchofjesuschrist.org/study/general-conference/1995/10/swallowed-up-in-the-will-of-the-father?lang=eng.

Mayo Clinic. "Depression and Anxiety: Exercise Eases Symptoms." September 27, 2017. https://www.mayoclinic.org/diseases-conditions/depression/in-depth/depression-and-exercise/art-20046495.

McConkie, Carol F. "Here to Serve a Righteous Cause." October 2015 general conference. https://www.churchofjesuschrist.org/study/general-conference/2015/10/here-to-serve-a-righteous-cause?lang=eng.

McGreevey, Sue. "Eight Weeks to a Better Brain." *The Harvard Gazette*, January 21, 2011. https://news.harvard.edu/gazette/story/2011/01/eight-weeks-to-a-better-brain/.

McKay, Brett and Kate McKay. "Got Thumos?" *The Art of Manliness*, March 11, 2013. Last updated June 6, 2021. https://www.artofmanliness.com/articles/got-thumos/.

McKeown, Greg. *Essentialism: The Disciplined Pursuit of Doing Less*. New York: Crown Business, 2014.

Mental Health Foundation. "How to Look After Your Mental Health." Accessed July 27, 2021. https://www.mentalhealth.org.uk/publications/how-to-mental-health.

Mental Health Million Project 2021. "Mental Health Has Bigger Challenges Than Stigma." Sapien Labs. https://mentalstateoftheworld.report/wp-content/uploads/2021/05/Rapid-Report-2021-Help-Seeking.pdf.

Meroney, John. "'World War II Isn't Over': Talking to *Unbroken* Veteran Louis Zamperini." *The Atlantic*, November 11, 2014. https://www.theatlantic.com/politics/archive/2014/11/world-war-ii-isnt-over-talking-to-unbroken-veteran-louis-zamperini/382616/.

Mims, Bob. "Mormon Sculptor Pours Her Passion and Pain into a Monumental Display." *The Salt Lake Tribune*, June 21, 2017. https://archive.sltrib.com/article.php?id=5345866&itype=CMSID.

Mindel, Nissan. "The Meaning of Prayer." Chabad.org, accessed March 23, 2022. https://www.chabad.org/library/article_cdo/aid/682090/jewish/The-Meaning-of-Prayer.htm.

Morin, Amy. *13 Things Mentally Strong People Don't Do: Take Back Your Power, Embrace Change, Face Your Fears, and Train Your Brain for Happiness and Success*. New York: HarperCollins Publisher, 2014.

Morin, Amy. *13 Things Mentally Strong Women Don't Do: Own Your Power, Channel Your Confidence, and Find Your Authentic Voice for a Life of Meaning and Joy.* New York: HarperCollins Publisher, 2019. Kindle.

National Alliance on Mental Illness. "Mental Health by the Numbers." Last updated March 2021. https://www.nami.org/mhstats.

Nelson, Russell M. "A Plea to My Sisters." October 2015 general conference. https://abn.churchofjesuschrist.org/study/general-conference/2015/10/a-plea-to-my-sisters?lang=eng.

Nelson, Russell M. "Closing Remarks." April 2019 general conference. https://abn.churchofjesuschrist.org/study/general-conference/2019/04/57nelson?lang=eng.

Nelson, Russel M. "Let Your Faith Show." April 2014 general conference. https://www.churchofjesuschrist.org/study/general-conference/2014/04/let-your-faith-show?lang=eng.

Neufeld, Gordon and Gabor Maté. *Hold On to Your Kids: Why Parents Need to Matter More Than Peers.* New York: Ballantine Books, 2014, 20–24.

Newton, John. *Thoughts Upon the African Slave Trade.* London: Printed for J. Buckland, in Pater-Noster Row; and J. Johnson, in St. Paul's Church-yard, 1788; Internet Archive. https://archive.org/details/thoughtsuponafri00newt/page/n3/mode/2up.

Nielsen, S. Gifford. "This Is Our Time!" April 2021 general conference. https://www.churchofjesuschrist.org/study/general-conference/2021/04/33nielsen?lang=eng.

Noble, Elizabeth and Leo Sorger. *Having Twins and More: A Parent's Guide to Multiple Pregnancy, Birth, and Early Childhood*, 3rd ed. New York: Houghton Mifflin Company, 2003, 120.

Oaks, Dallin H. "Recent Events Involving Church History and Forged Documents." *Ensign*, October 1987. https://www.churchofjesuschrist.org/study/ensign/1987/10/recent-events-involving-church-history-and-forged-documents?lang=eng.

Oaks, Dallin H. "The Desires of Our Hearts." BYU devotional address, October 8, 1985. https://speeches.byu.edu/talks/dallin-h-oaks/desires-hearts/.

The Official Anais Nin Blog. "Who Wrote "Risk"? Is the Mystery Solved?" March 5, 2013. http://anaisninblog.skybluepress.com/2013/03/who-wrote-risk-is-the-mystery-solved/.

Pascual-Leone, Alvaro, Nguyet Dang, Leonardo G. Cohen, Joaquim P. Brasil-Neto, Angel Cammarota, and Mark Hallett. "Modulation of Muscle Responses Evoked by Transcranial Magnetic Stimulation During the Acquisition of New Fine Motor Skills." *Journal of Neurophysiology* 74, no. 3 (1995): 1037–1045.

Pearce, Virgina H. "Prayer: A Small and Simple Thing." BYU Women's Conference, April 28, 2011. https://womensconference.ce.byu.edu/sites/womensconference.ce.byu.edu/files/virginia_pearce.pdf.

Peterson, Marlene. "WEMH #7 Notebooking." *The Well-educated Mother's Heart.* Podcast audio, August 17, 2017. https://www.librariesofhopestore.com/podcasts/wemh-7-notebooking.

Pinborough, Jan Underwood. "Elder F. Enzio Busche: To the Ends of the Earth." *Ensign*, February 1985. https://www.churchofjesuschrist.org/study/ensign/1985/02/elder-f-enzio-busche-to-the-ends-of-the-earth?lang=eng.

Poets.org. "Elizabeth Barret Browning." Accessed June 30, 2021. https://poets.org/poet/elizabeth-barrett-browning

Poirier-Leroy, Olivier. "How Michael Phelps Used Visualization to Stay Calm Under Pressure." YourSwimBook, accessed February 17, 2021. https://www.yourswimlog.com/michael-phelps-visualization/.

Pope, Conor. "Inside the Dark Web: The Truth Is There Is a Lot of Evil Out There." IrishTimes.com, October 13, 2018. https://www.irishtimes.com/culture/tv-radio-web/inside-the-dark-web-the-truth-is-there-is-a-lot-of-evil-out-there-1.3653092.

Quote Investigator. "If I Shoot at the Sun, I May Hit a Star." November 20, 2012. https://quoteinvestigator.com/2012/11/20/shoot-at-sun/#note-4805–19.

Quote Investigator. "Resentment Is Like Taking Poison and Waiting for the Other Person to Die." August 19, 2017. https://quoteinvestigator.com/2017/08/19/resentment/.

Radcliff, Deb. "Protecting the Mental Health of Cyber Warriors." Sans.org, October 30, 2019. https://www.sans.org/blog/protecting-the-mental-health-of-cyber-warriors/.

Renberg, Charlene. "A Testimony Through Song." Y Magazine, Summer 2013. https://magazine.byu.edu/article/a-testimony-through-song/

Renlund, Dale G. "Unwavering Commitment to Jesus Christ." October 2019 general conference. https://www.churchofjesuschrist.org/study/general-conference/2019/10/16renlund?lang=eng.

Rowling, J.K. *Harry Potter and the Prisoner of Azkaban*. New York: Scholastic Inc., 1999.

Royds, Kathleen E. *Browning and Her Poetry*. London: George G. Harrap & Co., 1923.

Sandberg, Sheryl and Adam Grant. *Option B: Facing Adversity, Building Resilience, and Finding Joy*. New York: Alfred A. Knopf, 2017.

Sax, Leonard. *Boys Adrift: The Five Factors Driving the Growing Epidemic of Unmotivated Boys and Underachieving Young Men*. New York: Basic Books, 2016.

Scott, Richard G. "Healing the Tragic Scars of Abuse." April 1992 general conference. https://www.churchofjesuschrist.org/study/general-conference/1992/04/healing-the-tragic-scars-of-abuse?lang=eng.

Seneca, Lucius Annaeus. *Letters from a Stoic: All Three Volumes*, translated by Richard Mott Gummere. Enhanced Media, 2015. Ebook.

Seow, Seraphina. "Feel Like You Don't Enjoy Anything Anymore? There's a Name for That—and You Can Break Through It." *Real Simple*, November 18, 2020. https://www.realsimple.com/health/mind-mood/anhedonia.

Shenk, David. The Genius in All of Us: Why Everything You've Been Told About Genetics, Talent and IQ Is Wrong. The United States: Double Day, 2010.

Sorenson, Aaron. "Prolific Composer and Songwriter Janice Kapp Perry Awarded Honorary Doctorate Degree." BYU News, April 23, 2020. https://news.byu.edu/character/prolific-composer-and-songwriter-janice-kapp-perry-awarded-honorary-doctorate-degree

South African History Online. "Mohandas Karamchand Gandhi." Last modified October 9, 2020. https://www.sahistory.org.za/people/mohandas-karamchand-gandhi.

The Stanford Prison Experiment. "8. Conclusion." Accessed July 14, 2021. https://www.prisonexp.org/conclusion.

Stepping Stones. "Bill's Story." Accessed October 15, 2021. https://www.steppingstones.org/about/the-wilsons/bills-story/.

Storey, Benjamin and Jenna Storey. "Podcast #701: Why Are We Restless?" Interview with Brett McKay. *The Art of Manliness*. Podcast audio, April 19, 2021. https://www.artofmanliness.com/character/advice/why-are-we-restless/.

Stowe, Charles Edward. *Life of Harriet Beecher Stowe Compiled from Her Letters and Journals*. Boston: Houghton, Mifflin and Company, 1890; Project Gutenberg, 2004. https://www.gutenberg.org/files/6702/6702-h/6702-h.htm.

Szabo, Ross and Melanie Hall. *Behind Happy Faces: Taking Charge of Your Mental Health, a Guide for Young Adults*. California, Volt Press, 2007.

Taylor, Bill. "What Breaking the 4-Minute Mile Taught Us About the Limits of Conventional Thinking." *Harvard Business Review*, March 9, 2018. https://hbr.org/2018/03/what-breaking-the-4-minute-mile-taught-us-about-the-limits-of-conventional-thinking.

Tedeschi, Richard G. and Lawrence G. Calhoun. "Posttraumatic Growth: Conceptual Foundations and Empirical Evidence." *Psychological Inquiry* 15 no.1 (2004): 1–18. https://doi.org/10.1207/s15327965pli1501_01.

Ten Boom, Corrie. *Clippings from My Notebook: Writings and Sayings Collected*. Minneapolis: World Wide Publications, 1984; Internet Archive. https://archive.org/details/clippingsfrommyn00tenb.

Ten Boom, Corrie, John Sherrill, and Elizabeth Sherrill. *The Hiding Place*. New Jersey: Chosen Books, 1971.

Twenge, Jean M. "The Age of Anxiety? The Birth Cohort Change in Anxiety and Neuroticism, 1952–1993." *Journal of Personality and Social Psychology* 79, no. 6 (2000): 1007. https://www.apa.org/pubs/journals/releases/psp7961007.pdf

Utah Department of Health. "Health Indicator Report of Suicide." January 5, 2021. https://ibis.health.utah.gov/ibisph-view/indicator/view/SuicDth.AgeSex.html.

Vinson, Terence M. "Meekly Placing Our Total Trust in God." BYU devotional address, February 11, 2020. https://speeches.byu.edu/talks/terence-m-vinson/meekly-placing-our-total-trust-in-god/.

The Wildlife Center of Virginia. "Human-imprinting in Birds and the Importance of Surrogacy." Accessed June 29, 2021. https://www.wildlifecenter.org/human-imprinting-birds-and-importance-surrogacy#:~:text=Imprinting%20for%20wild%20birds%20is,adult%2C%20providing%20them%20with%20safety.

The Washington Post. "Olympics 2012: Michael Phelps Has Mastered the Psychology of Speed." YouTube video, 3:22, June 15, 2012. https://www.youtube.com/watch?v=Htw780vHH0o.

Wang, Yuhwen. "The Ethical Power of Music: Ancient Greek and Chinese Thoughts." *Journal of Aesthetic Education* 38, no. 1 (2004): 89–104. Accessed June 29, 2021. doi:10.2307/3527365.

West, Thomas G. *Plato's Apology of Socrates: An Interpretation, with a New Translation*. Cornell University Press. https://www.sjsu.edu/people/james.lindahl/courses/Phil70A/s3/apology.pdf.

Wilcox, S. Michael. *10 Great Souls I Want to Meet in Heaven*. Salt Lake City, UT: Deseret Book, 2012.

Ziglar, Zig. "Your life is a result of the choices you have made. If you don't like your life, start making better choices." Facebook, December 8, 2013. https://www.facebook.com/ZigZiglar/posts/10152064931912863:0.

Acknowledgments

This book would not have come into existence without the help of many individuals. Thank you to Megan Roxas for encouraging me during a pivotal moment and giving me the feedback I needed to take the manuscript to the next level. Thank you to Kaylee Mason for being a very patient editor and working with me to get my manuscript ready to query. Thanks to the team at Cedar Fort for giving me this opportunity, specifically to Angela Johnson for patiently answering my newbie questions, for Shawnda Craig and the design team for creating the best cover design ever imagined, and for Heather Holm, Kimiko Hammari, and the editorial team for making every last detail look great.

Thanks to my mom for believing a book was possible even when it was just an idea in my head, for always encouraging me to go after my dreams no matter how crazy or unlikely, and for spending the last month of my pregnancy bunked in the nursery reading over drafts and combing through citations while waiting for babies to arrive. Thank you to my beautiful children, Clavin, Oliver, Everett, Harvey, and Maverick. You have filled my life with more joy than I ever thought possible. Finally, thank you to Taylor, my *media naranja*, for joining me on each crazy adventure and through every ebb and flow.

I would be remiss not to acknowledge the help of my Heavenly Parents and Jesus Christ in this process. Often, when it seemed I was making no progress, words would appear on the page as if by magic. If there is any good in this book, it is thanks to heavenly aid.

—Notes—

—Notes—

—Notes—

—Notes—

—Notes—

About the Author

Susie McGann has a master's degree in TESOL (Teaching English to Students of Other Languages) and has taught English language learners for the last fifteen years, including international students in the Marriott School of Business and in the Department of Student Development at Brigham Young University. A self-help enthusiast, Susie believes the power of the gospel is the key to living a deliberate life. From living abroad in her twenties, to obtaining her graduate degree as a young mother, to world schooling her five children, Susie has consistently tried to live her life on purpose and encourages you to do the same. Connect with Susie online at www.susiemcgann.com or on Instagram: @susiemcgann.

Scan to visit

www.susiemcgann.com